Why Missionaries Quit
Proven Tips for Longevity

AUTHOR: Dr. Tom Latham

EDITOR: Dave Carlson

DynoTech Publishing, Colorado Springs, Colorado, USA

Edited and published by Dave Carlson at DynoTech Publishing, Colorado Springs, Colorado, USA.
(www.dynotech.com)

This book is based on a doctoral dissertation "Missionary Problem Areas," Copyright © 1987 by Harry T. Latham. Used with permission.

Scripture quotations are from the King James Version (KJV) of the Bible.

ISBN: 978-1-885708-27-4 (Paperback)
        978-1-885708-28-1 (Hardback)
        978-1-885708-29-8 (E-Book)

Library of Congress Control Number: 2026909627

Print information is available on the last page.

First Printing: May 2026

Contents

Please refer to the index at the end of the book as a roadmap for quickly locating specific topics.

The Great Commission

And Jesus came and spake unto them, saying, All power is given unto me in heaven and in earth. Go ye therefore, and teach all nations, baptizing them in the name of the Father, and of the Son, and of the Holy Ghost: Teaching them to observe all things whatsoever I have commanded you: and, lo, I am with you always, even unto the end of the world. Amen.

Matthew 28:18-20

INTRODUCTION

Fourteen years as a missionary have shown me the urgent need to share my experiences with other missionaries and those considering this path. The casualty rate is too high. I have seen some missionaries last only a few months, others have never returned for a second term, and two couples, who were personal friends, quit after six years. The cost is too high and the need too great for such unreasonable casualties.

The major challenges facing missionaries (and, perhaps YOU) are sixfold:

1. They must adjust and adapt to the culture,

2. They must maintain and repair personal relationships,

3. They must develop a position on working with people with low incomes,

4. They must be faithful in soul-winning among all classes,

5. They must not release the church until it is properly prepared, and

6. They must maintain a warm relationship with their spouse and family, if they have them.

The chapters of this book clarify some of the problems missionaries face and offer practical solutions. Planning for the future is essential, and that future begins the moment a missionary arrives. While first impressions can be strong and sometimes misleading, I have outlined these situations to encourage change; if that doesn't happen, the missionary must adapt to meet them.

I have tried to stay positive, but our problems are creating more problems. Most missionaries can handle their blessings; it is their trials that will put them on the plane home. At times, the missionary's problems will have nothing to do with his being an American. The nationals are also suffering under the same system. At times, the nationals will suffer more easily, as their temperament traits may lend to the patient type.

Being informed is the best preparation. The missionary must shed idealistic dreams and be ready for reality upon arrival. Success or failure will depend on many factors discussed in this book.

AUTHOR NOTES:

The contents of this book remain essentially the same as the original doctoral dissertation I wrote in 1987. However, an additional 40 years of experience, living the contents of this book, has given me further insight into some of the concepts presented. I have updated some language to better fit the 21st-century context. I also use comparisons of costs between Brazil and the USA in 2026 US dollar values, instead of the original 1987 values.

The original dissertation, a major writing project, was submitted to the graduate division of Luther Rice Seminary in partial fulfillment of the requirements for the Doctor of Ministry (DMin) degree, which I was awarded in 1987.

Throughout the book, I generally use masculine pronouns. I refer to missionary teams, on the field, as husband-wife-kids family units, reflecting the typical (but not all) Baptist missionary culture of the 1980s. This is not meant to exclude others—please adjust pronouns as you read. I apologize if this offends.

My predominant experience is in Brazil, so many of my examples are specifically Brazilian. However, it should be easy for you to imagine similar issues in other cultures. The purpose of the stories is to give you insight into overcoming (marginally acceptable) or adapting to (best) cultural differences.

I am a Fundamental Baptist Christian. My doctrine, theology, and practice are reflected throughout this book. My views are guided by my understanding of the Holy Trinity: Father, Son, and Spirit, as well as God's Word, the Bible. My preference is the King James Version (KJV).

This book will be more informal than the academic dissertation that spawned it. The intent is to provide you with a helpful reference instead of a formal treatise. I will loosely follow a modified American Psychological Association (APA) style, but evoke "poetic license" when I feel it suits the subject matter. I will use APA inline citations instead of footnotes to acknowledge those who came before me and shared their ideas with the world. I will identify specific King James Version (KJV) Bible references in parentheses with italics, instead of citing page numbers in a specific Bible.

Several of the quotes I use from other authors contain grammatical errors, but I will show the quotes to you as I extracted them from the original source. I understand the academic requirement to use the Latin term [*sic*] to indicate that I have found an error in a quoted passage, so I don't get "blamed" for the error. But, since this book is informal and not a "graded school assignment," I will not point out the errors I noticed. (Feel free to do that yourself.)

If you are a professional reviewer, I understand you will do your thing. I am a professional writer, and I have done my thing. I trust you will enjoy the unique writing that makes me, me.

A missionary, especially during the early stages of his ministry, must adapt and adjust to become a "Jack of all trades," and do everything himself.

Image generated by Artificial Inteligence (AI).

CHAPTER 1
Culture Shock vs Adaptation and Adjustment

Introduction - Definition

Culture shock is the reaction you experience when you see a cockroach crawling over your dish of ice cream or discover a rat has eaten through the screen door, climbed into the crib, and chewed away the baby's pacifier. Experiences such as these would be shocking enough in the homeland, but to have them happen regularly is indeed a trying ordeal.

Culture shock is not limited to a day, a week, or a year. It is actually a state of mind that must be overcome to be a long-term missionary. The generally-accepted idea of culture shock could be pictured as a new missionary with his eyes "bugged out" as he tries to suffer through another ordeal! You may very well encounter frightful and disgusting experiences, the likes of which you could not have dreamed. Rather than enduring through the cultural differences, you must adapt and adjust. If you do not, you may find a bitter, complaining attitude developing, or you may buy a one-way ticket back home.

The kinds of experiences previously mentioned are those that cause screams and disgusting looks, both of which can be detected and despised by the nationals.

Extreme Reaction

The reaction to the initial shock may be so strong that the missionary will be disillusioned and, within a week, return as a failure. This reaction is usually caused by:

1. An idealistic approach to the missionary's spirituality, overcoming any situation.

2. An unwillingness to lower one's cultural barriers of both the body and mind.

3. Improper indoctrination concerning the actual conditions of the exact field.

4. A critical attitude rather than a helpful spirit from the veteran missionaries.

A more refined definition of culture shock is the emotional disturbance that results from encountering cultural differences in the environment. It is caused by the loss of familiarity with one's surroundings. It may result in strain, uneasiness, emotional maladjustment, and even failure. Some never recover, and they return to their homeland. Others doubt their call to the ministry, especially in missions. They blame God for making a terrible mistake by putting them on the mission field. Some reject the board, field directorship, and fellow missionaries, blaming all for a lack of orientation. A few have even caused great strife among the missionaries and nationals, thus hindering the work more than helping it.

Some missionary appointees are taught about culture shock, but actually experiencing it can be quite a trying ordeal. It may include the shock of:

1. Not being understood. (This is a new experience, and it is especially trying in a difficult situation.)

2. A drastic weather change. One might leave Minnesota in January and go to a place where the temperature is 100 degrees every day of the year.

3. Immediate dysentery from a food or water change.

4. Experiencing situations of which you have never heard of, let alone seen.

5. Paying 2-5 times the U.S. price for an inferior product that will break soon and for which you cannot get parts.

Adaptation and Adjustment

To many, culture shock has always been understood as a short period, usually one day to six months. It has a more lengthy influence that could be called "adaptation" or "adjustment."

This adaptation is a long process that may well extend the missionary's entire life. Some survive the initial shock but fail in the complete adjustment. There are many areas in which a missionary must constantly change, thus enabling him to remain on the field and return to it.

A well-adjusted missionary is a marvel to behold. His actions and attitudes have been molded to fit the customs and culture of his adopted land. Some missionaries are so completely adapted that they feel more at home on the field than they do in their homeland. Proper adjustment involves personal denial and control of temperament and stress, none of which is easily attained.

Proper adjustment will involve a denial of your personal rights of:

1. Being completely understood or having it your way, even though your way may be the right way.

2. Privacy.

3. Political involvement, including voting rights.

4. A middle-class standard of living.

5. A good education for your children.

6. A means of recourse when you are cheated.

One needs humility that allows them to acquiesce, even when they know they are right. This involves a willingness to admit when you are ignorant or wrong. It also helps in this area if you realize that it is not necessarily wrong to be different.

It would sound logical to think that a missionary was well-adjusted after four years on the field; that he had little left to change. Most missionaries arrive on the field with 25-30 years of home culture ingrained into their lives. Ethnic groups around the world testify to the difficulty of changing ingrained cultures. A missionary would be better prepared if he understood that there are some unchangeable cultural patterns he will never comprehend. He might go to his eternal reward before he can adjust to them.

Controlling temperament and stress is necessary for proper adjustment. Every missionary has a special personality and a God-given temperament. Controlling this temperament should be the spiritual goal of every conscientious child of God, and especially of the foreign servant of God. He is in the thick of the battle, being observed day and night as a witness to the reality of life under the control of the Holy Spirit. Excusing one's bad behavior by blaming a temperament trait or saying, "That is just the way I am," is common but totally unacceptable in the light of biblical truths.

One's behavior is usually strained to the limit by stress, and no greater stress may ever be experienced than that of living in a foreign culture. The amount of stress one encounters will vary depending on numerous factors. The stress chart shown on the next page will help explain the problem.

Stress-Producing Factors in Cultural Adjustment

$$\frac{A + B + C + D}{E + F + G + H} = \textit{Amount of Cultural Stress}$$

(Dye, 1974, pp. 61-77)

NEGATIVE FACTORS
A = Involvement in the Culture
B = Value of Differences
C = Weather and Frustrations
D = Uncontrolled Temperament Traits

POSITIVE FACTORS
E = Acceptance of Cultural Differences
F = Communication of the Problem
G = Emotional Security
H = Inner Spiritual Resources

Stress Chart

The purpose of the chart is to show that increasing any factor on the bottom (Positive) will reduce the amount of stress. And an increase in any of the factors at the top (Negative) will increase the level of stress.

Reducing stress is an important factor in the continuation of a missionary's ministry. His longevity is a tremendous contributor to the stability of the work.

Fatality Rate

The thousands of dollars spent to get a missionary to the field represent a tremendous investment. One example easily demonstrates that it could cost up to $70,000 just to put the missionary on the field. During his first term, a missionary could easily spend over $200,000 to maintain his family and work.

If one were to fail or quit, could it not be considered a sin, especially when it happened because of a lack of dedication or a humble spirit?

In a 1940 survey of 6,000 missionaries, 9% withdrew in the third year and 34% between the third and fifth years. It seems that the first term is very critical.

The investment cannot be taken lightly. The foreign missionary must be sure of his calling, and once sure, he must not allow anyone or anything to deter him from the completion of the will of God. The devil will do anything and use anyone (even Christians) to keep the missionary off the field.

First Impressions

Most new missionaries have never traveled outside the continental United States. They may have seen many slide presentations and, to some degree, even studied the conditions of their newly adopted land. Two things a slide presentation does not give are smells and experiences. Two requirements for successful missionaries are: no sense of smell and a large sense of humor.

> *Mission fields are not exotic, and the pictures one can find in the National Geographic magazines will in no way reflect truly what the missionary will find when he arrives at the place of his service. Beginning with his departure from the homeland, the missionary will need to make adjustments. But when he finally arrives on the field, he is faced with the immediate problem of making a series of adjustments so profound that his way of life will be altered beyond the imagination of the uninitiated. (Lindsell, 1955, p174)*

Everyone is going to face culture shock in varying degrees. One's reaction will determine how long he may stay or how effective he will be. A missionary may move from one extreme to another, but happiness and complete adjustment are found only in a correct balance. Although both extremes on the following chart are wrong, they have

Cultural Adjustment

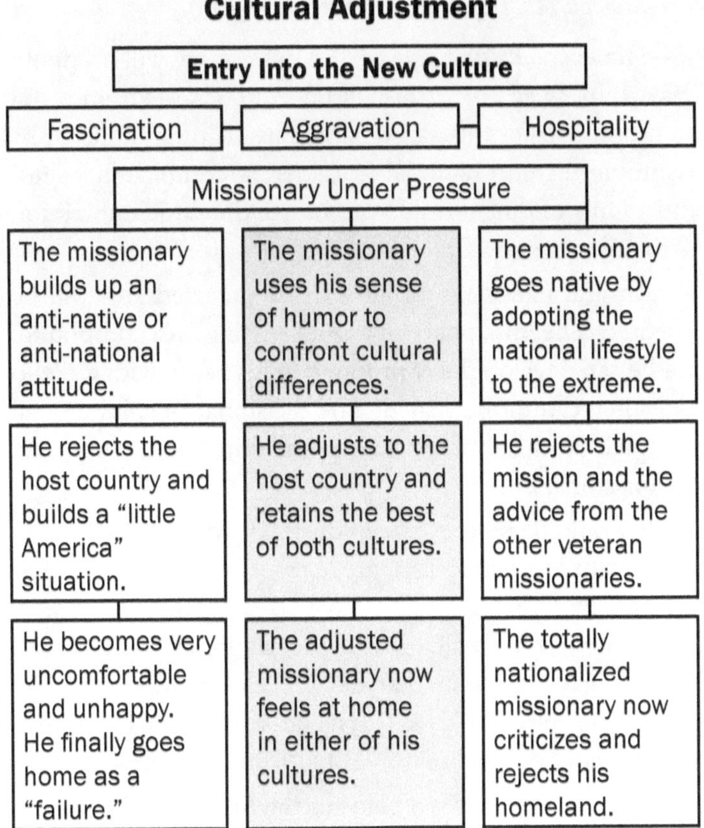

been practiced by well-meaning missionaries.

Little America Extreme

The little America extreme has been practiced more frequently in the past than it is at the present. Some old mainline, denominational missionaries and medical stations may still operate like this.

Gone forever, no doubt, is the forbidding wall of the compound designed to keep out all but those admitted by the gatekeeper. The church has become mobile, and politicians know that missionaries must get to the people. But they also know that there are limits to how far this can be accomplished. (Lindsell, 1955, pp. 155-156)

The evangelistic heart of the missionary will no doubt drive him away from this "little America" extreme. But he can construct this same barrier in his own home or by assuming an anti-national attitude. A complaining spirit and a fault-finding attitude can create the same impression as the old compound.

An anti-national attitude can be detected and will be resented. The missionary may not be living on a compound, but he can develop the compound in his heart, with walls so high they cannot be scaled. The missionary's children will also pick up this attitude and repeat things that embarrass the missionary.

It would be better to keep quiet. If one cannot control their attitude, silence is a great asset when one is upset or tired. It is better not to have to say you are sorry. A missionary who really loves the nationals will try to live in such a manner that he won't need to continually excuse himself and seek forgiveness for offenses he has committed.

One will never win a place in the hearts of the people with whom God has chosen him to labor by expounding phrases such as:

1. "That is not the way we did it in the U.S."

2. "You ought to learn how to do it right from me."

3. "What a dumb custom!"

4. "Can you believe how ignorant some people are?"

5. "All you nationals are _______." Any insult can be put into the blank. They have all been used.

The nationals may very well criticize their own country, and they often do, but to have a foreigner degrade one's fatherland is not so easily accepted. Basically, this is what the "little America" extreme· is saying, whether in the compound or in the complaining, criticizing attitude. An offended local citizen is more difficult to bring to Christ.

Going National

The other extreme of "going national" can be just as harmful, perhaps more so, to the missionary's longevity.

... Some people expect the missionary to "go native." By this, they mean that the missionary should so identify themselves with the people that they will eat their kinds of food, wear their kinds of clothing, and live in their kinds of homes. Living like a national is frequently deadly to the missionary. To eat like a national, forgetting the basic facts of hygiene, and to consume food that is foreign to taste and digestion, and without enjoying the immunity which comes from generations of resistance to germs and diseases, is fatal. (Lindsell, 1955, pp. 155-156)

Some have taken this matter of "going national" as a sign of spirituality or dedication. They think that by taking this step down the economic ladder, they can more easily reach the common people. Eating the food, drinking the water, and arranging housing equal to the common people may not open the door to anything but a "Pandora 's box." Some must weigh very seriously whether the Holy Spirit is leading them to endanger their family's lives and risk the end of their ministry by deciding to live like the nationals, especially when it is not at all necessary to have a fruitful ministry.

The Lord may very well direct one to preach the gospel in an underdeveloped or contaminated area, and by so doing, spend the life of His servant. David Livingstone, John and Betty Stam, William Borden, and the five missionaries to the Aucas illustrate this point. This kind of sacrifice must be directed by the Lord rather than by glory-seekers wanting to become self-appointed martyrs.

There is certainly nothing spiritual about wasting your life by means of carelessness and laziness on the altar of self-esteem.

> *"No child of God should feel at liberty to disregard what he knows to be the rules of good health, just because he feels like it, much less the man or woman on the mission field."*
> *(Williamson, 1957, p. 37)*

The nationals are always trying to climb the social ladder. They work hard and make sacrifices to give their families a higher standard of living and healthier conditions. Only the most selfish individual would require the missionary to endanger his health or life by insisting that he live as the nationals live. In some parts of the world, the missionary would actually "lose face" by adopting certain practices of the nationals.

Cultural Balance

The happy medium must be found if the missionary plans to reach the common people and maintain a prolonged ministry. Setting aside personal rights and accepting national ways that do not violate health or good biblical principles has been the path to the greatest success.

Hudson Taylor experienced this as he pioneered the custom of using Chinese attire. His acceptance was complete and unique. Dressing like the nationals is not really a difficult thing today. Missions have changed a great deal. In most major cities of the world, Western attire and, to some extent, Western culture are now practiced and accepted.

Unfortunately, there is class discrimination in most third-world countries. This is neither just nor biblical. The missionary cannot expect to change this system beyond his own converts, and even then, it is a great challenge that will tax all his diplomatic abilities. These class barriers are so strong and ancient that the missionary will do well to exercise prudent judgment rather than to try to westernize these nationals. Our job is to preach the gospel and to treat each person as an equal. It is the Holy Spirit Who must break down the wall of partition and make all men equal through Christ.

About 85% of nationals are of the poorer class. The missionary can easily retain his healthful, comfortable standard of life and still reach these people. The general rule is that the upper class will not lower its position, but the lower class will rise to a higher level if they are not made to feel unwanted.

"Going national" will not permit the missionary to minister to the upper class. If he maintains at least a middle-class standard, he can easily minister to all the classes if he keeps his heart right before the Lord. The change to national ways do not have to be a trial.

The new worker at his first station often goes through a stage in which he finds everything uncomfortable, unattractive, and difficult, but there is no need for him to become discouraged. The change comes slowly, and the young missionary may not be able to see it for a long time, but if he everlastingly keeps at it, he will surely find that after a few years, familiarity has made the difficult easy. Most people will also find that it has even made the distasteful pleasant. (Williamson, 1957, pp. 20-21)

Stages of Crisis

There seem to be various stages of crisis in a missionary's life. Possibly, these could also be called levels of dedication. At each level, there is a decision to be made. The decision will alter that Christian's future and affect the quality and/or quantity of the missionary force for years to come.

Infatuation

This stage could begin as early as the beginning elementary years, when the child responds to the feeling of being a foreign missionary. It is very common for younger children to experience this stage at Bible camp. This stage happens to anyone who feels God calling them to the mission field, at any age.

It is an imaginary romance, with possible sacrifice, danger, and intrigue, drawn from the experiences of serving in a foreign, possibly hostile, land. Almost everyone who ends up on the mission field has experienced these same feelings, though only about 1% of those who have experienced them eventually will end up on the mission field.

Confrontation

This stage is when the young person (usually a high school or college student) begins to count the cost of foreign service. Perhaps they are engaged to someone who is not interested in missions, or they have been offered a comfortable job in the homeland. The devil will sometimes occupy the life of the child of God with something good, causing them to miss what is the perfect will of God.

This stage is particularly dangerous for one who has been called to be a missionary and knows it for certain. When he is offered a good-paying job in a comfortable church, he is certain that after a few years as a pastor, he will answer the call to the foreign field. Some who make this decision never do leave for the field.

Deputation

After having been appointed by some mission board, the dedicated missionary must now begin a campaign to convince the churches, his colleagues, acquaintances, and anyone who will give him an ear that he is worthy of their support. This trying stage may take two to three years of phone calls, letter writing, and living out of a suitcase. It is a time of proof-testing. Does the candidate have the tenacity to finish the job? This experience will fortify him for worse experiences on the field.

It is the uncertainties and sacrifices of these seemingly unprofitable years that keep many possibly good missionaries off the mission field and in the homeland. One has to have quite a self-motivated personality to survive the rigors of 100,000 miles of traveling to unknown churches, located in strange, unfamiliar cities, where the reception may not be that which the young missionary had expected.

Indoctrination

The missionary has now arrived on the field. He has achieved the goal for which he prayed and sacrificed for years. The long years of education and trials of deputation have now culminated in his arrival on the field.

These first six months are critical. The new missionary work will probably lose its effervescent glow during this time. After the first case of infection and the first time he is cheated, he will begin to see the realities.

This is the period of culture shock at its worst. It is the awakening to stark reality. Before, the bugs and lice were just good illustrations; now they are constant companions. Some missionaries only last a few days, while it may take at least six months to do others in!

The new missionary has just missed the "Super Bowl," and his team was playing. He missed the class reunion and Christmas with the family. If he can survive the first six months, he will probably finish his first term.

Saturation

The missionary has now been on the field for three and one-half years. He has almost got a work going, but it needs a little more time. His furlough is coming due, and he has a longing to see green grass and "golden arches." His craving for the familiar things of the past seems to grow stronger every week.

Perhaps he has not been the tremendous success he once thought he would be. The nationals have not thronged to his message, as he had hoped. His wife is unhappy, and his children are tired of being away from familiar things and relatives.

Has God really called him to this work? If God has, why haven't there been more results? He doesn't feel like a David Livingstone or William Carey. Perhaps he made a mistake in choosing this kind of service. When he goes home, he will communicate to the mission board that he feels the Lord could use him more at home, to promote missions.

Termination

There is a final crisis that every missionary faces. It occurs at the sixth year of service. Why would a missionary quit after six years? There is not a lot of information written on this stage of crisis, but since we have passed our sixth year, we have concluded that missionaries quit because:

1. They are discouraged about the results they have experienced. Paul started over 100 churches, and they have only started one weak one. Perhaps the money given to support them could be used more effectively somewhere else.

2. They have encountered some difficult interpersonal problems with some missionaries and nationals. These offenses were not handled biblically and, therefore, were never resolved. There doesn't seem to be any hope of improvement in these areas. He would rather choose his own co-workers.

3. Many areas of the culture offended him, and he had misguided aspirations that things would eventually change. Yet after six years, he sees that things are not going to change. The culture is ingrained in people's personalities, or possibly a result of their personalities at work. They are satisfied with living this way. He can't stand it any longer. They can have their culture and customs! He is going home, where things are operated with organization, logic, honesty, and confidence.

4. He is just tired, tired of missing his family reunions and favorite sporting events (he never liked soccer anyway). He is tired of flies and cockroaches, parasites and worms that crawl under his skin, smells and pollution, dishonesty and lies, and high prices and poor quality. He is tired of small churches, few men, low-grade music, and casualness about sacred things. He is tired of dealing with people of low standards who won't follow his advice. He is hindered by a low-income congregation that can't even buy its own Sunday school material.

That is why he is now packing his bags to return to the homeland in the middle of his second term. This disillusioned missionary is now ready to call it quits. He is not the pioneer church-planter he once thought he was. Not all is lost, though. His six years on the mission field have provided him with some great sermon illustrations!

Living Conditions

The following specific examples of cultural problems have been drawn from our fifteen years as foreign missionaries. Some of them are particular to the field where we serve, but we have heard missionaries from other fields express the same experiences and frustrations. These illustrations are not intended to slander any particular field or nationality, but to better prepare the prospective missionary by forewarning him.

The Climate

The climate can easily exaggerate everyday living conditions. Not all mission fields are hot! Because the largest number of unreached people live in the tropics, most missionaries work in hot, tropical climates. The cultural problems, plus the struggle with the language, are augmented by the strain of the heat on your physical system. Protecting yourself from the heat is not a matter to be taken lightly. The use of fans and air conditioners is becoming more common in many of the hottest fields.

The hotter the climate, the more sensitive you are to the diseases that thrive in these tropical areas. The bugs multiply rapidly, and viruses seem to travel in the very air you breathe. Skin problems are common, and you spend most of the time you're infected trying to figure out what bit you! Your first national friend will probably be the pharmacist.

Public Transportation

A taxi can be rather expensive if you do not know the most direct route to your destination. You may sometimes discover that the agent at the bus station made a mistake on your ticket. Because you lack the means to prove you are right, you pay twice. Willingness to admit fault is rare, and the usual axiom, "The customer is always right," does not prevail. It is not uncommon for a bus that holds 45 people to have 100 passengers, with the extra 55 standing in the aisle and someone sitting on your arm.

Depending on how far you ride into the interior, you will find dogs, cats, and even chickens as regular traveling companions. On the crowded buses, it is important to keep your elbows tucked in and your wallet in your front pocket. It is easy to get your handbag sliced and lose your official documents.

Property Rights

Property rights are vague in most countries. Some areas still respect squatters. One can claim land by just occupying it for a specific time. People may dump their garbage, sand, rock, or wood on your sidewalk or in the road, causing you to traverse around it. Your neighbor may run his sewer water into your yard or onto your sidewalk. If someone hits your car, you may have a difficult time collecting even if you can prove that he was 100% wrong. In most countries, there would be no authority to determine fault, and sometimes just being a foreigner means being in the wrong. As soon as your accent is heard, the dollar signs begin to appear as you are considered to be rich (*Aren't ALL Americans rich?*). In some countries, insurance is not required, so driving defensively is very important.

Hiring Personnel

Hardly a week goes by without someone knocking at your door asking for work. You must always settle on the price of work to be rendered before the project begins. A clear understanding of the quality of the work must also be agreed upon before starting. All questions about clean-up and dissatisfaction should be settled before the work begins. It is not a matter of lacking faith in the nationals, but rather of allowing yourself the option to direct the work rather than letting the situation rule you.

The missionary should not pay for the work until it is finished. You should not put large sums of money for purchasing materials into others' hands. Rather than this, you should accompany those purchasing the material. This is the usual procedure. It is expected; if not followed, it can cost more than a friendship!

The missionary would do himself a favor by not

hiring believers. Usually, believers are hired because the missionary/pastor wants to help them and hopes that they will do the work for the church or pastor more cheaply than others would. If something unexpected happens, the missionary could very well lose that believer, even though it was not anyone's fault.

Obtaining the fair price of tips is a must in each new locale where the missionary travels. Even after being a missionary for years, you can still be cheated and fooled by some people. It is a culture with standards different from those you are used to, which makes the problem more difficult than you might imagine.

Paying Bills

Payments are made at the bank. You may encounter long lines. After spending 20 minutes in line, you find out that you are standing in the wrong line. This causes a great deal of frustration. The man in front of you may have $1,000 in change and small bills to be counted right there at the cashier's window. After waiting an hour in a line three blocks long, you become impatient and begin sending crowders to the back of the line. It is not just a matter of getting your bills in the mail and writing checks to be mailed. All payments must be made in person. In our country, it is against the law to send money through the mail.

Thinking Processes

Understanding the national's way of thinking is a challenge to the new missionary. It is not something that can be learned in a short period of time. Sometimes a national will tell you what you want to hear and not necessarily the truth. When you order something, it may not be delivered by the promised date. You must keep on top of the situation at all times. Delays do not usually occur from a lack of concern or laziness, but from a lifetime of living in a culture where time is not as important as it seems to the Westerner. At first, you think that you are being treated this way because you are an American. After a while, you learn that the nationals treat their own people the same way.

Completing tasks is not easy when you deal with a system that operates on bribes or the "tomorrow" policy. If you want t o talk to the boss, he may be out. According to the employee, he will be right back! Just wait and be patient, even if it takes half a day. (After wasting several hours waiting, you learn to return later or another day.) Sometimes there is only one man who can handle your problem. He is not available because he went to the interior to visit his uncle's sister's sick brother-in-law!

The Barter System

Bartering is not my favorite method of doing business. You can generally begin by reducing the marked price by 50-60% and start bartering from there. If you do not soon develop a hard bargaining attitude, you may very well get "ripped off." When you do, there is no Better Business Bureau to help.

In the States, you might barter for a house or for a new car. On the mission field, you could barter for carrots. Even after years on the field, the barter system is still a thorn for the timid buyer.

Transit Authorities

Transit authorities may operate quite differently from what you have ever experienced. Police officers are standing on the corners of the streets, ready to copy your license plate number if they feel you have violated a law. You will have to pay the tickets before you can receive your new car tags. You could very well have three to seven tickets for violations that you did not know about.

Although you may not be able to remember when or where you violated a local law, and even though they may not have the specific infraction noted, you must pay. This is a system that Americans will have trouble adjusting to because they have been used to a more just way. Don't despair. Your national friends are suffering under the same system and don't like it any more than you do!

Highway Courtesy

Common highway courtesy is not known in most foreign countries. The exhaust pipes of diesel trucks and buses come out at the bottom of the cab. When following closely behind a bus or leaving a stopped position adjacent to a truck, your car is flooded with black smoke and fumes that choke you. These fumes can severely irritate your eyes and cause significant discomfort for people who wear contact lenses or have allergies.

Being run off the road by a truck passing a bus on a hill is more than a common experience, even more so when you are riding a motorcycle.

Saving Face

Allowing the national to save face is very important. It is exceedingly difficult at times, especially when the truth is apparent or important. Without any previous experience, the missionary must perform this proficiently, or he may cause a problem that could hinder the work for years. Allowing the national an opportunity to save face is more important than proving you are right (concerning non-biblical issues).

Various Other Problems

Other varied problems may include: breaking teeth on white rocks hidden in the rice, chasing geographical worms under your skin, finding lice in your hair, having your children susceptible to worms and parasites, and having most minor cuts become infected, encountering tarantulas, snakes, flies, mosquitoes, and cockroaches year-round, and being victimized by a variety of bugs whose names you cannot even find in the annals of science.

Language Problems

Incentives and Discouragements

Americans can travel 3,000 miles across our great land and still speak their mother tongue. There really is no incentive to learn different languages. In Europe, you may travel only 100 miles and encounter another language. This proximity necessitates studying the neighbor's language.

Most Americans have a mental handicap against learning any foreign language. Because of this handicap, many missionaries arrive on the field knowing very little about the language-learning principles. If the missionary wants a lifetime ministry, the language must not be just studied; it must be mastered. If God has called the missionary to a certain field, He will give that person the ability to learn the language. Some will have more ability than others. God has given many women a natural ability with languages. It is common for a sincere but insensitive national to say, "Did you know your wife speaks the language better than you do?"

At first, the missionary will be too timid to speak, but as he overcomes this fear, he will enter the experimental stage. Studying a new language may be quite different from what the missionary could imagine. He cannot just attend an hour-long class and then forget it all until the next class. He must take what he has learned and put it into practice to buy his bread.

The missionary would have to have been born on the field to speak the language without an accent. Just a short visit to the home of a long-term foreigner in the United States will prove that the missionary will always speak with an accent.

No long-term personal relationships can be established without learning the national language. Personal counseling and evangelism would be severely limited without speaking the language. It would also be an affront to the pride of the nationals if they were constantly forced to deal with the missionary through an interpreter.

Although some missionaries definitely do not have much ability with languages, there is really no excuse for speaking the native tongue poorly. Diligent study will enable anyone to speak sufficiently. Ability is not the greatest gift—to plod and persevere is the key. Even a cursory study of linguistics will show that progress comes in stages. It is not necessarily the talented missionary who will excel, but the one who, through trial and discouragement perseveres.

Superseding Language Importance

There are missionaries who, although they can speak the language even better than the nationals, lack a fruitful ministry. Showing genuine Christian love to the people is more important than speaking the language. One missionary who had served in Brazil for 24 years definitely did not speak the language well. One national commented concerning him: "We know he does not speak our language well, but we know that he loves us." Three of the seven national pastors in the state had come from his ministry.

Understanding what the national is really saying will take years of experience. Just knowing the language does not mean that you will understand what they are really trying to communicate.

When Abraham haggled with Ephron about the burial place of Sarah, it appeared as though Ephron really did want Abraham to take the land without payment. Abraham knew the people's character, and he did not think for one minute that the land was being offered freely (*Genesis 23:13-20*). Abraham paid the full price because the offer was only a customary gesture. This same gesture is practiced in countries today. When you visit a home and admire a picture or household item, the usual response is: "Take it, it is yours." This is merely a customary gesture, not a valid invitation to back a truck up to the house and help yourself to anything that catches your eye.

Stages of Language Development

1. Anticipation. You are willing to learn a language. This is an important attitude. Some will not even consider becoming missionaries because they are too fearful or too lazy to learn a foreign language.

2. Humiliation. You begin as a child. It is very embarrassing to speak worse than a two-year-old. Even the children make fun of you. All your pride is gone.

3. Communication. This stage is the language on a limited basis. You speak in short phrases, but you are thrilled to be understood. You can now buy bread and find out the time.

4. Expression. You can now express yourself in ideas and communicate your opinions. You can now start witnessing.

5. Exhaustion. This stage involves despondency in trying to be understood and understanding what the national is really trying to say. You have finally come to realize that you will always speak with an accent and, therefore, always be known as a foreigner. If you don't pass this point, you will probably quit. Rest and recreation, with spiritual emphasis, are greatly needed.

6. Comprehension. You have now passed the simpler conversational level. This is necessary to reach the upper class. You begin to understand what the national means and what he is saying.

7. Relaxation. You have reached a comfortable level of expressing yourself. This is contentment with measurable progress.

8. Animation. You are now at the level where you can take pleasure in using their idioms and gestures. You now begin to translate all your American jokes.

9. Nationalization. This is the point where they ask you where in Brazil you were born. You are now considered a Brazilian. Wherever you go, people tell you that you. speak just like they do. This is reached by only 0.001% of the missionary force, and only after they have spent 25-30 years on the field. Pride is a problem at this stage. Unfortunately, you are about to retire. When you have finally gotten your act together, the curtain begins to fall.

Church Differences

Having been raised in a certain culture for thirty years or more has implanted within each missionary a definite pattern of Christianity. This pattern may not be duplicated anywhere in the world. Even small things, such as singing in tune with accompaniment and going out with friends for an ice cream after church, may not be experienced by the missionary on the field. Although he may not consider himself a patterned culturist, the missionary has practiced certain things that will be missed.

Just the appearance of the meeting place will be a contrast. One could leave a carpeted, air-conditioned sanctuary on one Sunday and (the following Sunday) find himself sitting on the floor in an open-air grass hut, knocking bugs off his legs, straining to cool himself with a makeshift fan, and trying desperately to occupy his mind since he cannot understand a word being said.

There will be new songs to learn and usually a new pattern of worship, which may include practices that the new missionary may not understand the value of. One may even disagree with the tempo of the music or the dress permitted for church worship.

The struggle does not end with merely conditioning oneself to these ways of worship. The struggle continues as you ponder just how much of this system needs to change to create an atmosphere conducive to worship while still retaining a national identity.

There could be much confusion in the services as local children walk in and out at will. Even people of your own church may leave the pew to get a drink or to spit out the window. Bats flying through the church during the service will greatly detract from the preaching.

In the southern missionary fields, many churches have adopted the common philosophy that time is unimportant. Therefore, everyone starts late. You can determine to stop this by starting on time, but after you sing so many solos, you will probably conform. You can improve this problem by announcing you are going to start a half an hour earlier. Weddings are famous for starting 90 minutes late, or more.

Government Dealings

Rights and Politics

Americans are accustomed to working with a government that usually operates in the realm of truth and follows a policy of honesty. United States citizens have always been able to call the right department and have something done. If the process is too slow or the outcome is unjust, complaining to the right authorities and even appearing on TV can sometimes resolve the situation.

When you arrive in a foreign field, you have left your

citizenship rights at home. You must now consider yourself a citizen of only the heavenly kingdom. Your pleas for justice and equity may only have an ear at the throne of grace.

The missionary has no legal rights in foreign countries. The country where you serve may be a dictatorship, and your presence in that country may be a delicate affair. Certainly, God never called a missionary to be thrown out of a country because he was politically rather than spiritually involved.

Paul served the Lord during a time of severe persecution. You may look diligently in the writings of all the New Testament authors and never find anything but admonitions to give honor· and respect to political leaders. The gospel should not be confused with ideas of revolution. The missionary's message is substitutionary, not revolutionary. He does not need to bring the wrath of the government down on his head.

Bureaucracy

On the foreign field, you must deal with a bureaucracy. Some of them will be very complicated. One part of the government may deceive the other, catching the missionary in the middle, wondering what to do, who is right, and where to go from here. At times, the process is slow. It seems as though you must fight "tooth and nail" to get the slightest thing accomplished. If you try to speed up the process, you may entice the wrath of an official, and things could slow down or stop. Invariably, when you want to see an official, he is gone, and no one else can solve your problem. You cannot leave legal matters in the hands of others. You must walk from station to station, day by day, until you achieve your goal.

The government may not feel responsible to the people. If the city breaks your sidewalk while repairing the street, it may be your responsibility to pay for the sidewalk repairs. You may phone to complain every day for a month, but the guilty party no longer works there. The buck will always be passed. It seems that the workers call the boss "irresponsible," and the boss calls the workers "donkeys," leaving you in the middle as the loser.

Inflation

Inflation and poverty are essentially government problems. When a country's inflation rate reaches 125% or more a month, it becomes very difficult to do anything with the believers' tithes. When interest rates are 18% per month, it is impossible to borrow money to build churches.

The missionary is surrounded by poverty. It is a government problem when no help is available. This only affects the missionary when he constantly encounters beggars at every turn. The missionary does not want to be hard, but giving money to beggars is to see it go up in smoke or go to the liquor industry.

Incentives (Bribery)

The missionary may find himself in a situation where a bribe is requested, if not verbally, then by the mere fact of a delay. His convictions are screaming "NO," but the situation is desperate. Remember, "It is never right to do wrong," and God is bigger than any situation. God may have created the situation to test your faithfulness. To begin a habit of paying bribes is to open a "Pandora's box." When it is known that the missionary will pay bribes, some will create situations to make a gain.

This is not a new problem for missionaries. When Paul was in Felix's jurisdiction, he was able to give his defense as recorded in *Acts 24*. He was not released, as Felix was hoping to get a bribe.

Conclusion

A majority of the missionaries who quit do so for two reasons: either they cannot adjust to the culture, or they have personality problems with other missionaries or nationals. In a survey taken among the leading mission boards, it was discovered that of all the missionaries who quit, 25% quit for health reasons, 11% quit because of problems in the immediate family, 5% quit because of marital difficulties, and 24% quit because of personal problems. The personal problems included the following: bitterness, divisions, discouragement, dishonesty, immorality, lack of discipline, lack of dedication or submission, not accepting criticism, uncooperative spirit, problems in doctrine, difficulty in language adaptation, interpersonal problems with other missionaries or nationals, and problems adjusting to the culture or climate.

The survey shows that just as many people quit for personal reasons as for health problems. These facts should make the missionary aware of the dangers. This adjustment and adaptation take a long time. One-term missionaries attest that it is a serious problem. The best sight is foresight, and in this matter of cultural problems, one would do well to prepare oneself. The missionary might better prepare himself by:

1. Reading missionary biographies and articles on cultural shock, or even visiting the field itself.

2. Praying for strength to accept and adjust to the cultural differences.

3. Understanding that many unpleasant things will never change, no matter how long he waits.

4. Accepting the fact that in some areas it will be very difficult for him to change.

5. Understanding that to be different does not mean

to be wrong.

6. Realizing that the American way to do something may not be the only good or right way to do it.

7. Knowing your weaknesses and depending on your strengths.

8. Understanding that adjustment at any level will require humility and effort, it doesn't come easy.

9. Praying the serenity prayer: "Lord, grant me the serenity to accept the things I cannot change, courage to change the things I can, and the wisdom to know the difference."

Whosoever cometh to me, and heareth my sayings, and doeth them, I will shew you to whom he is like: He is like a man which built an house, and digged deep, and laid the foundation on a rock: and when the flood arose, the stream beat vehemently upon that house, and could not shake it: for it was founded upon a rock. But he that heareth, and doeth not, is like a man that without a foundation built an house upon the earth; against which the stream did beat vehemently, and immediately it fell; and the ruin of that house was great.

Luke 6: 47-49

Dr. Latham's first church in Mossoró, Rio Grande do Norte, Brazil.

MOSSORÓ CITY COAT OF ARMS

CHAPTER 2
Missionary Interpersonal Relationships

Introduction - Relationships

Missionary Casualties

Fractured interpersonal relationships are at the top of the list of reasons missionaries quit and never return to the field. For this reason, it is of utmost importance to study and resolve these problems.

Unless a missionary makes a good psychological adjustment to the foreign environment, culture, and working relationship with his fellow missionaries, his service will be of limited value. Longevity is essential because the initial investment in a missionary is extremely high. If a missionary stays only one term or less, the investment has been too high for the meager return. It takes a whole term to:

1. Accept and adjust to cultural differences.

2. Make worthwhile contacts.

3. Learn the language well enough.

From the very start of his missionary career, the servant of God must maintain good relationships. The sphere of fellowship on the mission field is limited; therefore, interpersonal relationships are easy to strain and important to maintain. He must maintain good relationships with the board, the field director, his co-workers, his supporting churches, his correspondents, the nationals, and his own family.

Areas of Pressure

The following areas of pressure are common in most mission fields. These are listed in the order of their severity. Having difficulty in:

1. Showing patience toward nationals.

2. Maintaining regular personal Bible study and prayer.

3. Reacting to a government official's inefficiency and obstinacy.

4. Overlooking others' weaknesses.

5. Adhering to a program of mental stimulation.

6. Reacting to an unusually strong sinful environment.

7. Discussing matters with missionary companions, who hold conflicting views.

8. Maintaining warm spiritual fellowship with fellow missionaries.

9. Following a regular daily schedule.

10. Being generous with fellow missionaries with different ideas and methods.

All of these areas seem rather insignificant in light of the great task before the missionary. However, still in the flesh, we must face our personalities and deal with each fault according to the leading of the Holy Spirit, being daily directed by the Word of God.

Pressures and tensions in any work situation (even in America) disturb, distract, and dissipate an individual's emotional and mental energy. Temperament make-up, not environment or circumstances, is the primary factor in tension. Although climate or culture may cause trying situations, the answer to adjustment and happiness comes when the missionary walks daily with the Lord and is controlled and changed by the Holy Spirit.

Spiritual Weaknesses

Much difficulty could be avoided if the missionary kept in touch with the Lord. If he neglects his devotions and prayer, the difficulties will increase, and the distance from the only source of power will be lengthened. The missionary must avoid a hurried, busy schedule, late hours, and constant hard work, which is often worse than it was in the homeland.

Habits need to be formed early. This devotional area is the core of a missionary's spiritual effectiveness. Problems can be avoided or kept small if this discipline is maintained.

A missionary's relationship with other Christians is directly proportional to his relationship with the Lord.

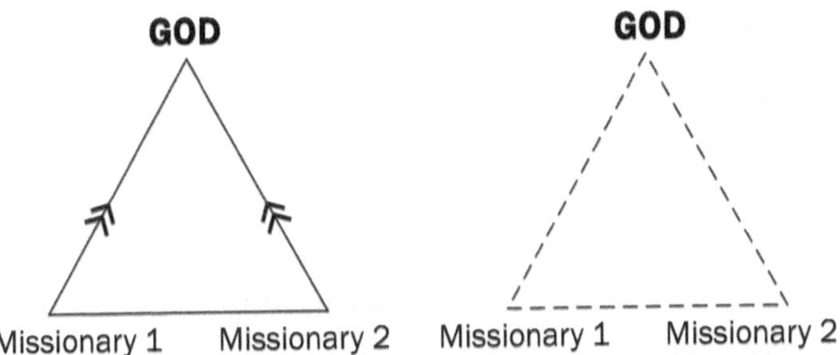

LEFT: The strength of the triangle is invincible. The closer each missionary moves toward God, the closer he is to the other missionary. (Sorley, 1963, N.P.)

RIGHT: A fractured relationship with God leads to interpersonal problems with others, including missionaries and administrative personnel.

Emotional Health

Increasing importance must be placed on the missionary's emotional health. To maintain emotional stability, one must accept constructive criticism, work happily with others, accept majority decisions, and adjust to physical conditions.

Some missionaries are very sensitive people. They are sensitive to the voice of God and to the needs of the heathen. Therefore, they become more vulnerable to fractured personal relationships and experience great personal pressure on the mission field.

Many United States companies have begun to recognize the importance of their workers' emotional health. A great deal of time and money has been spent to identify potential problem areas and how to avoid them. Unfortunately, little has been researched on the work and problems of the missionary. Some missionaries are thrust into working situations they cannot handle, compounded by the climate, culture, and language; this added emotional factor may be the straw that breaks the camel's back!

Idealism Versus Realism

Most interpersonal mismanagement stems from people living in an idealistic rather than a realistic world. Much can be passed off as bad organization, but usually, in the area of missions, bad interpersonal relationships are not caused by disorganization.

Very little is done to prevent interpersonal problems. Why is this so? It is because many have idealistically concluded that any Christian should be able to get along with any other Christian. Theoretically, this is true. But the missionary does not live in a world of theory. He lives in a world of heat and cold, hunger and sickness, sorrow and pain, sinners and carnal Christians.

Missionaries have long been held up as the most spiritual of the saints. Just because one can minister on foreign soil does not make that person more spiritual. Any missionary can be very carnal and unspiritual, walking in the flesh rather than in the Holy Spirit.

The mere fact that one is a missionary will not give one patience, tact, or poise. If one is not patient, tactful, or easy to live with in New York or Chicago, he certainly will not be in Hong Kong or Mexico City. The truth is that a missionary will be under greater stress on the foreign field than he ever would be at home.

The Bible has a great deal to say about personal relationships. Each of the following verses uses the phrase 'one another': "Love one another" (*1 John 4:7*); "Prefer one another" (*I Timothy 5:21*); "Be in subjection one to another" (*Ephesians 5:21*); "Be kind one to another" (*Ephesians 4:32*); "Forgiving one another" (*Ephesians 4:32*).

Relationships Between Missionaries

The Personal Life

Problems arise when the missionary is thrust onto a field where his personality, ideas, and philosophies may stand in sharp contrast to those of his fellow workers. Unlike most pastoral situations in the United States, a missionary may not be able to choose his co-workers. A pastor working in the States would never call an assistant who greatly differed with him in philosophy or practice. If he found his new pastorate staffed with personnel incompatible with his personality or plans, he would soon make some changes.

A missionary does not always have the privilege of choosing his co-workers. This is especially true for missionaries in agencies with a conventional structure and that rely on large governing bodies. Although some of these agencies may allow the missionary to choose his area of service, they insist that he work together with other missionaries he does not even know.

Although one may not be able to choose their fellow

workers and thus avoid a great many problems, one can choose their mission agency. There are only a few agencies that allow their missionaries complete liberty. The new missionary would do well to pursue a board that allows him this liberty.

The longevity of the missionary's ministry could well depend on how he relates to the mission agency. One can change agencies, but this usually results in a loss of forty to seventy percent of support. It could involve one to two years more of deputation work to recover this lost support. This period away from the field could also result in the loss of visa privileges.

> *One-third to one-half of first-term missionaries do not return to the field for a second term. This mortality rate is not due to death alone but mostly to other factors. Ill health, inability to adjust to conditions on the field, psychological tensions, disillusionment, failure to learn the language, inability to get along harmoniously with colleagues, and dissatisfaction of the board itself with the services of the missionary are among the causes for mortality in the missionary ranks.* (Lindsell, 1955, pp. 161-162)

One can work with difficult people. Regardless of the agency, each missionary still has to work with people of differing personalities. Some weird people do make it to the mission field. Some of these people are going to be difficult to understand and handle, especially when one is also dealing with a cultural and language barrier.

In the finite wisdom of the missionary, he may think that God has chosen the wrong men for his co-workers or for administrative jobs. But God can either use these men to mold other men or even change these co-workers and leaders to conform to what He wants them to be. An intolerable situation may be just what God ordered for the new, inexperienced missionary. If it is handled properly, it could be a refining experience, making the missionary a rare jewel for future use.

God can change people. He has already changed many missionaries a great deal, or they would not seek to mend offenses biblically. Sometimes it is easier to be silent, hoping things will improve, or perhaps be forgotten. Sometimes it is easier to give the other person a "piece of your mind." But neither of these methods will produce a spiritual, workable situation with coworkers.

Trying to convince another missionary that he is wrong or offensive may be like trying to "turn back the tide" (*Galatians 6:1-3*), an exercise in futility. But biblical mandates must be followed if the missionary is to deal with problems and seek a cure for the wounds.

Situations may arise in which the present work and future success of the missionary are hindered or threatened, his convictions are violated, or his emotional condition is stressed to the limit. Something must be done. A situation causing these effects cannot continue without great physical or spiritual harm to the missionary and his work.

If any problem reaches the breaking point, the missionary might have to change his organizational connections. It should be stressed that no organization called the missionary to serve. Since it is God Who calls, then only God can recall. A missionary should not question his call just because he cannot get along with certain missionaries or office personnel. The missionary must be on his guard, for some in positions of leadership would try to convince him that he is not spiritual or qualified simply because he cannot get along with certain administrative personnel or missionaries.

Interpersonal conflicts are not new. Abraham parted ways with his nephew Lot because "there was strife between the herdsmen of Abraham's cattle and the herdsmen of Lot's cattle" (*Genesis 13:7*).

It would probably have been difficult for Paul to work with Peter, as they had very different personalities. Peter was a sanguine, and Paul a choleric. Paul even thought it necessary to publicly rebuke the wavering Peter for separating himself from the Gentiles (*Galatians 2:11-14*). This personal rebuke probably did not make a great bond of fellowship between these two Apostles.

Mark turned back from accompanying Paul on the first missionary journey. Paul didn't think the reason was valid and refused to take Mark on the second journey. Paul and Barnabas parted ways over Mark's usefulness. Perhaps Paul wanted Mark to prove himself at home first (*Acts 15:36-41*). Barnabas was Mark's uncle, and sometimes blood can be stronger than doctrine or good sense.

Mark was not going to quit serving the Lord just because Paul thought he did not meet the standard. Mark traveled with Barnabas. We do not know what happened to them, for the Holy Spirit chose to follow the ministry of Paul and Silas through the author of the book of Acts, Dr. Luke. Later, Paul recommended Mark, and he even said that Mark was profitable to him and his ministry (*II Timothy 4:11*). Mark never quit. God gave him the privilege of authoring the first gospel of the New Testament era!

Jacob's life is another example of God's training school. Jacob had deceived his brother twice and had to flee for his life. God directed Jacob to Laban, who cheated and deceived him on several occasions, enough to make Jacob change his ways. God gave Jacob, the "deceiver," a new name: "Israel, " meaning "Prince with God" (*Genesis 35:10*). One does not drown by falling into the water. He only drowns because he stays there. Some of God's greatest servants were men who had failed horribly in their spiritual life. This list includes Abraham, Moses, David, Peter, and many modern-day saints. There is only one thing worse than failure: quitting.

God can use failure to rid us of our pride and teach us to depend on Him. Failure can make one a better servant of God (if he allows the Holy Spirit to continue working in his heart). Sometimes God allows failure to make us better. He never intended it to make us bitter. If one turns bitter against those who have done him harm and refuses to forgive them, that bitterness will eventually turn against God. The spiritual descent will only get steeper and longer.

Problem Areas of Personal Conflicts

1. One missionary raised with a different lifestyle may not be able to accept the unwillingness of another to become involved in his interests and hobbies, such as planting corn in the front yard or attending sporting events.

2. A missionary coming from a low-income family background, who lives like the nationals, may criticize others for fancy belongings, expensive vacations, and extravagant church buildings. He may even chide his fellow missionaries for living too affluently and lacking true dedication.

3. One missionary may feel it is permissible to stretch the law to the limit, arguing that it is the law, but it is not enforced; therefore, he is free to do as he pleases. The old excuses of "Everyone is doing it," and "They can't arrest all of us," are sometimes used.

4. A missionary sells another missionary something at an inflated price, but it breaks. Another missionary gets upset because his fellow missionary won't sell him something at a low price. One rarely makes friends by selling to them or buying from them.

5. A missionary is invited for ice cream on Sunday afternoon. After spending two hours in the blazing sun, waiting outside a locked gate, he decides to go home. Three days later, he finds out that the inviting party was at the goat farm, petting the billies, and he could not get back in time!

6. One sure way to cause problems between missionaries is for them to tell each other how to raise their children. Unless counsel is sought, it usually is not appreciated and will be resented.

Conflicts In The Work

One missionary may not appreciate the way another operates his program or administers his church. Some have a definite inability to express their thoughts in a kind, constructive way. A quick temper or a sharp tongue can do a great deal of damage in planning sessions. An unwillingness to consider others' ideas may be very harmful.

A "ho-hum" attitude toward another's success can cause the enthusiastic missionary much discouragement. Failure to get excited about someone else's work and success is usually prompted by jealousy and a fear of falling behind. Some missionaries won't work together for fear that someone else will get the credit or glory.

A bitter, begrudging spirit toward another missionary can linger for years. This bad spirit can cause the camp to split into factions that pick at every opportunity to be different. Practicing the forgiveness of *Ephesians 4:32* will not only give the missionary a good night's sleep but will also heal the wounds on both sides. Missionaries have the capacity to forgive, but few really forget. Forgiveness includes forgetting. Being too sensitive and defensive adds to these problems, and an unwillingness to communicate forbids the chance of reconciliation.

Failing to consider the plans of the whole group has caused some missionaries to become islands and little popes unto themselves. The closing of weak works, or projects started on the "spur-of-the-moment whims" of one missionary, may cause a "black eye" for the whole movement. Independence in thought and action, though natural, can be detrimental and even dangerous to the good of the combined local effort. Selfishness is the greatest temptation, and humility the greatest need. Teamwork is vital even to the independent missionaries.

One missionary who is avidly anti-Calvinistic may be pushing people to make decisions. He may be picking green fruit while severely criticizing his coworkers, who may be dealing a bit more slowly with prospects and having far fewer casualties. It is a matter of theology that shows in day-to-day practice.

A missionary may be so well adjusted to the culture that he has adopted the slackard philosophy of his locale. Late arrivals, last-minute cancellations, hurried planning at the final hour, and inconsistency in general can cause two missionaries to part ways rather than unite their efforts.

Sometimes, when differences arise, the offense is not discussed, nor is reconciliation sought at the level of the offenders. Accusations to the mission agency or the field director are made, which leave the biblical pattern in Matthew chapter eighteen completely out.

Perfect Combination

Each individual must endeavor to understand others' talents and goals and allow them to develop their own ministry within the group's goals, without jealousy or criticism.

A perfect combination of personality characteristics could be:

1. <u>Availability</u> — Being ready to help in the area of another' s ministry, regardless of who gets the credit.

2. <u>Dependability</u> — Being able to be counted on to perform that which has been promised, even though it requires unexpected sacrifices.

3. <u>Flexibility</u> — Being able to adjust to new situations and problems without accusations or criticisms.

4. <u>Humility</u> — Being able to see the importance of the other person's talents and goals.

If these four personality strengths were exercised, most conflicts among missionaries would never occur. Problems occur because even though they are saved, the missionaries are still sinners. The old nature wants to act naturally, and the new nature wants to act spiritually. It is up to the missionary himself to determine which of the two natures will rule his personality and life.

Flexibility or Frustration

Any personal relationship will be exaggerated by cultural stress. Cultural stress will be further complicated by the inability or unwillingness to handle it. Inflexibility causes frustration and increases stress. For this reason, a study on the matter of flexibility or frustration is necessary.

Flexibility is the ability to adjust to new situations. It appears to be the most important of the four previously mentioned. Flexibility will defeat frustrations caused by interruptions. In a missionary's life, interruptions are normal and can cause frustration for the inflexible. One never knows when someone may drop in for a couple of days. Perhaps the busy missionary will be called to fill the place of a co-worker who came down with a sudden attack of a strange tropical disease. This opportunity will allow the missionary to practice "availability."

Seeing only one's own point of view will cause

frustration and stress for others. Each missionary has gifts and callings that differ. When co-workers are unwilling to compromise (not in biblical doctrine or practice) and adjust to work for the good of the whole group, this inflexibility will cause frustration and bitterness in them and others. This is when humility is necessary. Recognizing the importance of others will lead each missionary to appreciate others and work together to accomplish the group's goals. Even the most independent missionary has goals that require at least some teamwork.

The fear of failure can cause much anxiety. When the missionary has done his part in witnessing, praying, and pleading with love, he must leave the results to God, trusting Him to draw people to salvation by the Holy Spirit. God never fails, and He will bring people to Christ through the missionary if he has enough patience to wait. Frustration is the problem.

An unwillingness to accept cultural differences may cause much frustration. This is one of the key areas of testing, by both God and Satan. God tests the missionary to prove him, to make him a better servant. The Devil tests him to disapprove of him, to make him a bitter servant, and to drive him off the field.

One must accept other customs as equally right rather than a threat to his own customs and values. Some missionaries have a deep fear of losing their cultural heritage, especially for their children, who are usually more nationalized than their parents. One need not fear environmental adjustment. God has never expressed animosity towards any cultural system or custom that was not contrary to His Word or His nature. If the customs are contrary to God's Word, the missionary needs to teach the biblical way, with love and patience. Instead of becoming un-American as is feared, he is actually becoming a bi-cultural person. He then becomes a more useful minister. Understanding this will ease stress and, in turn, frustration.

Living conditions in certain areas of the world can be very primitive and difficult. A missionary who had never seen a cockroach could find one daily on his bed or table. They could be as big as his thumb. If he kills it, the meat-eating ants may haul them away before he finds time to dispose of it. The missionary may encounter tarantulas larger than softballs. Some of these unwanted creatures are even found in beds or dresser drawers. Fear of bugs, parasites, worms, rodents, and infection can leave a person constantly on edge.

Fighting Stress Caused by Frustration

When frustration strikes, stress becomes a problem. Even the spiritual missionary might find it hard to adjust or be flexible. If these sources of stress are not handled with flexibility, the missionary may even have a nervous breakdown. The frustrated missionary under stress must find a release for a time. He may improve the situation by indulging in light reading, basking in healthful music, participating in sports, pursuing a hobby, taking a vacation, riding a bicycle or a motorcycle, sleeping or resting, or taking a brisk walk. Sometimes the missionary is just worn out and cannot handle normal stress.

Relationships Between Missionaries and Agencies

Basic Organizational Systems

There are two basic organizational systems for work procedures. Every agency will operate under one of these two types, but there are many variations within each. For the sake of space, only the two most common types will be discussed.

The independent system allows the missionaries to

work alone, without restraints or organizational hindrances. There are many advantages to the independent system.

1. The independent missionary is not accountable to any other missionary or group of missionaries.

2. The independent missionaries do not vote in any way concerning the work or life decisions of others.

3. The missionaries are responsible only to the president of the mission and their field director, if they have one.

4. The administrative personnel in the States do not usually interfere with the missionaries unless they are violating biblical principles or mission policy.

5. Problems between co-workers are minimal. The worst interpersonal relationships they would face would also occur in every-day personal or secular work relationships.

6. If the independent missionaries working with the same agency do not get along, all they have to say is, "Fine, you go over to your side of town, or state, and I will work here." This is not an ideal situation, nor is it necessarily the will of God, but it does happen. Under this system, it may not mean the end of one's ministry.

7. If, for some reason, the independent missionary must change agencies, he will probably lose less support than he would if he were with a conventional agency. The conventional-type churches are very strong in supporting only missionaries from their approved agencies.

The conventional system requires all the missionaries in a given area to form a voting unit. This unit must approve each missionary's work. They, in turn, must have their decisions approved by the field director (a position to be described later). If any further decision is needed, the problem must go to the executive board and then to the full board. The local voting unit is called a field council. They usually meet two to four times a year for business and fellowship. The kind of authority they have depends on the hierarchical system that created them. Some field councils are only advisory to the missionary, and others do not allow their missionaries to make any major decisions regarding their work without the group's approval. It is easy to see how conventional groups such as Presbyterians and Methodists could fall into this type of operation, but how Baptists, who have been known for their independence, could operate like this is beyond belief.

Some missionaries claim that the strength of their work is because of the field council operation. Yet if it is examined according to the Bible and Baptist history, including polity, it would be found to be an unwarranted, unbiblical hindrance.

Nowhere in the Bible is there an example of pastors or missionaries grouping to decide on each other's work. In Acts chapter fifteen, the council only recommended some basic principles to the churches. Nowhere in the Bible can one find a group or an individual handing down orders to another person or group.

> *In this respect, therefore, and so far as their independency is concerned, Baptists are manifestly founded on the New Testament order of church building and church life; and, so far, are true successors of the Apostles. Nor does it avail to urge objections to this independency, or magnify the difficulties to which it is liable. It can be shown that other forms have inherent in them even greater liabilities to misuse; while this, if it were established by divine wisdom, must be the best fitted to its purpose and is the one to be used and preserved. (Hiscox, 1894, p. 159)*

Any organization must be operated loosely—like a

rope of sand. There is no fear of one group or one church controlling any other church or group of believers. Each church should be entirely independent of the others, and it must remain so. The same is true of the interpersonal relationship between the missionaries.

The usual appeal of this conventional system is that field council control is necessary on the foreign field. If it is unbiblical and against Baptist polity, how could it be necessary? There is not a single independent Baptist pastor in the United States who would operate his ministry under these conditions. He would be appalled even to think he had to get permission from his fellow pastors and their churches to operate his own work. This would be called conventionalism or dictatorship control. Yet, this is exactly the type of organizational control practiced by some so-called independent Baptists on the foreign field.

When politics enters the religious scene, there will always be problems. The administration of one's own life and his local church is difficult enough without being controlled by some outside force. Even more problems may occur when that governing body is not on the field, does not do the work, and may be populated by those with no experience. Experience does not necessarily make one a good administrator, but the lack of field experience will be a definite detriment to capable leadership.

When this political system is used, a great deal depends on two key people:

1. The <u>field council chairman</u> — He is usually appointed by the field director or elected by popular vote. He may have been chosen for the job just because no one else wanted it, rather than for his spirituality or ability to lead.

2. The <u>field director</u> — He is appointed by the president of the mission and approved by the board.

He usually has an office at the headquarters in the States. He may be experienced or not. He could also be a "yes-man" to the president.

These two men may have personalities that are not pleasing, nor are their actions controlled by the Holy Spirit. Either of them could be a legalist or extremist who could cause the work undue harm. When a great amount of authority is placed in the hands of one man, the work can be controlled by that man, whether he be spiritual or not.

One of the greatest problems with this kind of hierarchical leadership is a definite unwillingness to acknowledge administrative problems, shortcomings, or mistakes. When mistakes happen, leadership tends to follow humanity's general pattern: failing to admit being wrong for fear of losing credibility. Actually, the credibility level would probably rise with humble confessions.

Some leaders tend to refuse to look objectively at their own faults. Instead of sitting down and discussing the problems, the leaders support each other, whether they are right or wrong. This attitude causes conscientious missionaries to become despondent and either change missions or quit the mission force altogether. A leadership evaluation by the missionaries themselves would bring many of these problems to the forefront and allow for their correction. Instead, these problems go unaddressed, resulting in repeated mistakes and the unnecessary loss of good missionaries.

Leadership can place undue pressure on the missionary. This pressure usually comes down from the top. Perhaps the mission has not released enough churches to the nationals this year to justify its budget and the number of missionaries on the field. The annual meeting is coming. The pressure is on to make a good report. Therefore, the missionary is told to turn his church over to "some" national. The missionary knows that the only national remotely qualified would destroy his three years of work in three weeks. What should he do? Should he bend to pressure and sacrifice the permanent on the altar of the immediate? These are pressure situations that cause interpersonal problems.

The pressure to produce good reports for supporting churches and administrative leadership may lead the missionary to operate in a non-spiritual manner. The desire to look good may be stronger than convictions or kindness. The missionaries have to give monthly reports to the mission board and frequent prayer letters to the supporting churches. The missionary should not bend to these pressures. God is the real Judge of success. A truly spiritual missionary cannot sacrifice either biblical principles or important personal relationships for his desire for success.

A Proper Attitude

Whatever system the missionary works under, he can be a blessing or a hindrance. Which one he is will depend on his attitude. One attitude that will really help in either system is patience.

Most independent missionaries are self-motivated, or they would not have survived deputation. One of the greatest problems could be avoided if the new missionary were patient rather than rushing in to correct what he considers long-standing mistakes. Having just entered the new culture does not really give the "rookie" much in the way of foreign wisdom. The new missionary will probably save himself a lot of unnecessary criticism and strained interpersonal relationships if he listens rather than advising during his first few years. Some wounds he may inflict could very well never heal. Although some missionaries may be able to forgive, they may never forget, especially when the wounds seem to reopen with new offenses.

> *The novice must remember that he comes without benefit of previous experience. He is faced with a new set of circumstances which he does not understand. He will see gaps and defects in the pattern from the moment he commences his work. He will see places where he thinks immediate changes should be effected. He will fail to understand why certain things are done the way they are. He will be gripped by the disappointment of the slowness with which things are done. He wants to see results; through all of this he must recall that usually there are good and sufficient reasons based on long and painful experiences why missionaries do things the way they do. Second, he must remember that silence will be his best ally for the first year or two. (Lindsell, 1955, p. 186)*

In all that has been said up to this point, it should be added that the "lion's share" of the burden of a good working relationship lies at the feet of the veteran missionary, as he should have the greater maturity and experience. Sometimes the new missionary is so ignorant about what is going on around him that he doesn't even know the right questions to ask. It is the responsibility of the veteran to inform the new missionary, without the "rookie" having to ask or suffer as a result of this lack of information.

Relationships Between Missionaries and Nationals

Relationships With Unbelievers

The "gringo" has not always been well received in foreign countries. Nationals readily notice the flippant, superior attitudes of some American tourists. Because Americans have been accustomed to an organized structure and honesty as the best policy, they have little patience with other cultural patterns. Therefore, the missionary will already have to live down the reputation that Americans have abroad.

In dealing with unbelievers, the missionary must never feel that he can be unkind or rude to a national who does not live in his city or neighborhood. The missionary might think that he can be as forward as he wants because he will never encounter this person again, nor is he trying to get him into his church. This is sometimes the approach practiced by those who are ignorant concerning the whole plan of God.

God has used many to plant and many to water, and He gives the increase. Since a missionary is not the only one planting and watering, he must be careful lest he turn the national against the message of the gospel. The missionary may be only one link in a chain of witnesses that God will use to bring a national to Christ. If he offends the national, the chain may be broken. Every missionary could give an example of this.

There are some things in the culture and some customs that will really bother the new missionary. Americans are prone to making comparisons. Unkind statements only alienate the national from hearing the gospel. An American would feel equally insulted if he heard someone with a strong accent criticizing the United States. The patriotic American would respond by saying, "Why doesn't he just go home if he doesn't like it here"? And that is probably what nationals will be thinking, even though they may be too kind to say it. Local idioms and customs should be studied. Forgiveness and pardon should be practiced, even more so among unbelievers.

Missionaries react to loose morals up close. Drinking, gambling, low standards of living, and heathen religious practices will bother the missionary. Just living among non-Christians of other lands is difficult. Irritation or disgust at customs and practices, if not accompanied by deep compassion, will erect barriers and close doors of opportunity.

Relationships With Believers

A missionary's first personal relationship with believers depends on whether he starts a church from nothing or with believers, perhaps borrowed from another church. If he starts it with a few believers, he will have an immediate relationship to foster. The first thing any missionary will have to do is to demonstrate the love of Christ. This love can be shown without even knowing the language well.

If one is not too proud to learn, they can benefit greatly from national believers. Some of these believers have suffered persecution and been victorious. They have loved the Lord and tithed, even though they have not been greatly blessed financially. Some believers have suffered greatly in health and living conditions, yet they still praise the Lord. These are the kind of testimonies that can humble a proud missionary.

A bit of confidence must be placed in the hands of faithful believers. The work will never be nationalized unless the missionary trains and releases authority to national believers who have demonstrated faithfulness, even in difficult circumstances. Some of these believers run businesses and are leaders in the secular world; they surely have enough talent to run the work of God.

Criticizing one national to another will not build confidence in your leadership ability. The national knows that if you criticize others in front of him, you will also criticize him in front of others. Remember the "Golden Rule." It is a wonder that some nationals still love the Lord, considering how they have been treated by some well-meaning but ignorant missionaries, both rookies and veterans. Veterans can be just as guilty of allowing the natural man to control their temperament as rookies can.

Receiving Christ should make a difference in the manner of living for any national. On a percentage basis, no more of them live the Spirit-filled life than Americans do. It is always easier to be more severe of others than we are of ourselves. Missionaries also tend to blur the difference between cultural traits and personality problems.

Some countries may have long-standing habits of lying and dishonesty. When people get saved, it sometimes takes a while for them to understand that these things are not a regular part of life. Sometimes it has been forty years that one has been dishonest and lied their way out of every difficult situation. The national may call it something else other than lying (perhaps "inventing a story"), but it is still the same sin.

The missionary needs to have as much patience with these long-standing problems as God does with his long-standing faults. *Ephesians 4:32* is a key verse to this type of treatment. Impatience, cutting remarks, criticisms, and irritations have caused serious issues between missionaries and nationals. People must be loved where they are. The missionary must take these nationals from where he finds them to where Christ wants them to be spiritually.

Fundamental Baptists are not compromisers, but the adage, "When in Rome, do as the Romans do," will probably be good advice in the area of:

1. Being interested in the local affairs.

2. Reading the national or local paper.

3. Using local gestures and idioms.

4. Eating the local food and learning to like it.

5. Conforming to the local style of dress and order of services.

Repairing Broken Relationships

God forbid that one missionary should offend another. One would have to stick their head in the sand to keep from noticing that it does happen. If biblical patterns were followed to mend offenses, there would be far fewer disasters and more long-term missionaries.

The Bible gives steps for both the offender and the offended. Both have a responsibility before God to heal the broken relationship.

1. The offended is to go to the offender privately and try to explain the offense. If the offender will not hear him, the offended is to take one or two Christians with him when he confronts the offender the second time. If he fails to hear these brothers in Christ, the offender is to be taken before the church body. If he fails to heed the advice of the church, there is no higher appeal. He is then to be treated as a heathen (*Matthew 18:15-19*).

2. The offender is to leave his gift at the altar as he remembers he has offended his brother. He is to go to his brother and seek to have the wound repaired. The offense can only be properly addressed by confessing the wrong and asking for forgiveness. After this act of obedience, the offender may return to the temple and continue to offer his gift to God with a clear conscience (*Matthew 5:23-24*).

The ideal situation would be for both parties to meet on the way to each other, seeking to do their part to heal the wound. But even if the other party does not initiate action, one cannot wait; they must do their part.

Unfortunately, this pattern set down by our Lord is seldom followed. When a first-term missionary tried to approach a veteran about ongoing offenses, the field director told him he could not do it that way. It was explained that a "rookie" had no right to approach a veteran. The offended missionary was told that he would have to go through the field council chairman and through the field director. This pattern may appear to be a kinder way to do it, but it is not the way the Lord told the offended to do it. Circumventing biblical patterns will cause more problems than it can solve.

The **Field Work and Tensions** chart on the next page represents only the offended party's responsibility. In many cases, the greater responsibility lies with the offended missionary for no other reason than that some missionaries are insensitive and don't even realize they are offending anyone.

There are usually two extremes in handling offenses. The "heartburn" extreme is to <u>tell no one</u>, especially not the offender. The idea is: "After all, he has to come to me." This response only causes one to hold a grudge and to build up bitterness against the offender. This approach makes it very difficult for the offended one to live with. The offended party may develop an ulcer and may eventually have to return home because he made himself sick.

The other extreme is to <u>tell everyone else</u>, except the offender. This approach is more commonly called "back-biting" or "extinguishing someone else's light." However, when someone else's light is put out, the extinguisher's light is no brighter; in fact, it reduces the total amount of light. This method causes division and unrest among the believers. God has promised to destroy those who destroy His church (*I Corinthians 3:13-17*). The result of this approach will be to divide the missionary personnel into separate camps, cause ulcers, and possibly run others off the field.

The biblical pattern is to <u>tell God first</u>. The missionary must ask God to reveal any faults on his part, including bad attitudes. Ask God for an opportunity to approach the offender. Have a discourse with the offender and seek to mend the wounds with love and forgiveness. This process will help prevent ulcers already in the making and glorify

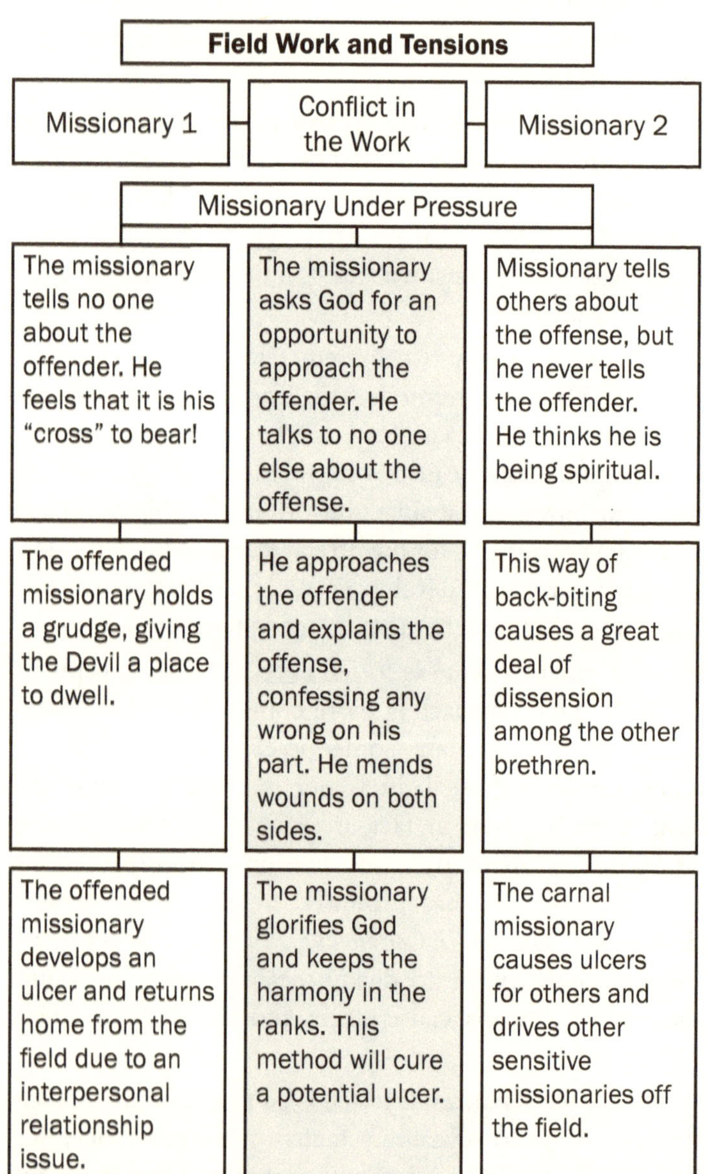

Field Work and Tensions		
Missionary 1	Conflict in the Work	Missionary 2
Missionary Under Pressure		
The missionary tells no one about the offender. He feels that it is his "cross" to bear!	The missionary asks God for an opportunity to approach the offender. He talks to no one else about the offense.	Missionary tells others about the offense, but he never tells the offender. He thinks he is being spiritual.
The offended missionary holds a grudge, giving the Devil a place to dwell.	He approaches the offender and explains the offense, confessing any wrong on his part. He mends wounds on both sides.	This way of back-biting causes a great deal of dissension among the other brethren.
The offended missionary develops an ulcer and returns home from the field due to an interpersonal relationship issue.	The missionary glorifies God and keeps the harmony in the ranks. This method will cure a potential ulcer.	The carnal missionary causes ulcers for others and drives other sensitive missionaries off the field.

God by bringing others to Christ.

Maintaining Good Relationships

The following are some good suggestions for establishing and maintaining good personal relationships in all areas of a missionary's life:

1. Everyone has a God-given, different personality, with certain strengths and weaknesses. Everyone usually has a pleasing personality, but everyone has a bad day now and then.

2. Be as willing to forgive as you have been forgiven.

3. Don't allow the sun to go down on your wrath, or don't hold a grudge.

4. Be as willing to learn, both from co-workers and nationals, as you are to teach.

5. Be quick to confess wrong on your part and slow to find it in others.

6. Do not allow others to fill your ears with gossip, whether it is true or not!

7. Be as patient with others as God is with you.

8. Do not make promises you cannot keep. If you keep people waiting, be sure to apologize. Don't fall into the "face-saving" habit.

9. Be as interested in the ministry and activities of others as you are in your own.

10. Control your temperament rather than having it control you.

11. Compliment people whenever you can, but do not flatter. Give a good report of all men. If you cannot give a good report, then refrain from giving any report, unless you are an integral part of either the problem or the solution.

12. Do not love people with an insincere concern. People who are hurting can detect insincere love. Love people because God loves them, not just because they might be able to do something for you.

13. Cry with those who cry and laugh with those who laugh. Do not belittle other people's feelings or problems. Be sympathetic to the sufferings of others, but be slow to burden others with yours.

14. Save your strength for the important battles. Satan would have you spend it on non-issues.

15. Do not criticize others unless you are willing to make some constructive suggestions. Always seek to be discerning rather than judgmental.

16. Tact is an artful gesture. Learn it and use it. Always seek to reprove (bring someone to conviction with love) rather than rebuke (sharply disapprove or reprimand).

17. Have a long fuse on the old temper bomb. The atomic bomb only explodes for a split second, but it brings decades of destruction.

18. Be more concerned about what God thinks of you than what your fellow missionaries may think. If you can please God, you will also please most of His spiritual children.

Conclusion

To see how important interpersonal relationships are, one need only converse with missionaries and ex-missionaries. The casualties are numerous, and the scars are still painful. It is an important part of the missionary life. It cannot be taken lightly.

Time does not heal all wounds, especially if further irritations reopen them. The only things that will heal interpersonal wounds are communication with the offender, resulting in a confession of wrongdoing, and a forgiving attitude on the part of the offended. A tolerable situation can result from only one of the above, but a spiritual relationship cannot be realized without both.

The work is too important to allow the missionary his personality quirks. Controlling his personality will be the most important thing a missionary can do. If he does not control his personality by the Holy Spirit of God, he may very well be asked to leave the field, or even worse, he could be the reason others leave the field.

The missionary is wrongly considered to be the most spiritual of saints. Yet this spirituality may operate only while he is on furlough. It is very important to impress the supporting churches. Unfortunately, some missionaries don't feel quite as concerned about their actions on the field, where the watchful eye of supporters cannot see them.

Every Christian ought to be careful in the areas of interpersonal relationships; even more so the foreign missionary, because so much is at stake for eternity.

Put on therefore, as the elect of God, holy and beloved, bowels of mercies, kindness, humbleness of mind, meekness, longsuffering; Forbearing one another, and forgiving one another, if any man have a quarrel against any: even as Christ forgave you, so also do ye. And above all these things put on charity, which is the bond of perfectness.

Colossians 3:12-14

Dr. Latham's second church in Restinga, Rio Grande do Sul, Brazil

RESTINGA CITY COAT OF ARMS

CHAPTER 3
Monetary Problems
Missionaries Face

Introduction - Love of Money

The Bible says that "the love of money is the root of all evil" (*1 Timothy 6:10*) and that it is the beginning of many sorrows. The purpose of this chapter is not to discuss the monetary needs of the missionary, but rather to explain:

1. How the natural living standard of the missionary may hinder his work.

2. How the missionary can build a church with the tithes of low-income people

3. How the missionary can show the love of God without causing dependency on him or his finances.

Most missionaries have regulated income both at home and on the field. While at home, they may live in modest dwellings, which may be provided. Certainly, most missionaries would be considered average, if not low-income, compared to professionals with the same education and experience. Unlike other professionals, missionaries are usually not paid more for earning more degrees or many years of experience.

The missionary is considered middle-class. This is the level at which most of his fellow Christians are. The scales used to determine standards of living in the United States and in any third-world country differ significantly. A middle-class American would be considered rich in most third-world countries. The missionary is not rich, usually never has been, and probably never will be. He may very well leave the missionary force at the same economic level where he came into it.

> *In general, the first principle which operates for the missionary is the principle that the financial return for his labor is not computed based on his intrinsic worth. It is not compensation for hours spent, skills involved, or years of service. Never is the question asked, 'What is he worth,' but rather, 'How much is the bare necessity for himself, his wife and children'? After forty years of service, he is no better off than when he first began. The novice just commencing to serve, begins where the veteran of forty years still is.* (Lindsell, 1955, p. 150)

When the missionary goes to the field, he may go to a large city such as Rio de Janeiro or Mexico City. Although there are some rich people in these cities, the majority are poor. For instance, Mexico City has a population of 21,000,000 people, of which 30% are at the poverty level. In Calcutta, India, 70% of the 20,000,000 inhabitants live in one-room houses, and 70,000 miserably poor people sleep in the streets. These conditions of poverty will stagger the mind of the new missionary.

A middle-class American usually owns a car, owns their home, rents a nice house, or lives in a comfortable apartment. He has a cellphone, and his children study in excellent surroundings. Most stateside Americans have come to expect these things as a regular part of life. The 2026 minimum US salary is $2,700 a month. In Brazil the average monthly income is $320 a month. Many Americans have never seen poverty, real dirt-poor, dirt-floor poverty.

On the average mission field the economic condition of the national Christian compared to that of the denominational or faith missionary is striking. In some places, indeed in many places, the possession of an automobile automatically places the possessor in the category of a wealthy man. According to the standards in the homeland the missionary is poor, but according to the standards of the "National Christian" he is quite wealthy. (Lindsell, 1955, p. 152)

The biggest problem the missionary will face is caused by semantics. The missionary needs to redefine his terms. Redefinition of terms involves trying to think as the national. It will be an exercise in futility to try to convince the national that the American missionary is not rich. At home, the missionary will encounter very few social-class problems stemming from his standard of living, but he may very well face difficulties on the field.

If the missionary has a need, he can write to his supporters and usually find a solution. The percentage of his wages used for necessities may be extremely lower than that of the national. A national may spend 80% of his income on food, whereas the missionary spends only about 15%. When a missionary buys a bicycle, he pays only about 2% of his monthly salary; therefore, it is an inexpensive purchase for him. The national will pay a month's salary for the same bicycle; therefore, it is a very expensive purchase. Sincere nationals may reprimand the missionary for saying that a certain item is cheap. Their response is: "It may be cheap to you, but it is very expensive for us. We had to spend a large percentage of our salary on that purchase."

Working With The Poor And Needy

Housing Difficulties

In choosing a location for his church, a missionary must consider his housing needs. If he locates the church in a lower-class area, where most of the population lives, it may pose a dilemma for him. He wants to be available to work, but he does not want to live in a lower-class area, especially since good housing is rarely available there.

One of the great attractions to rural work is that the cost of living is lower. Therefore, one can start a church more quickly because buildings and land will be less expensive. But the majority of the people live in the chief cities. If one wants to reach the majority, one must live in the crowded, polluted, and sinful cities.

Living conditions are very important to the longevity of the missionary's ministry. Comfort and security are of utmost importance. If his housing is not sufficient, his family may contract diseases, be unhappy, and even feel inadequate. Also, he will have difficulty ministering to the middle and upper classes. A poor person will accept an invitation to an upper-class home in a better-class neighborhood, but a middle-class or upper-class person will rarely enter a poor neighborhood.

Even without trying, a missionary's income has placed him in the rich class bracket of third-world countries. He is "rich" because his salary is ten to twenty times that of some of the people to whom he will minister. Although he may try to act genteel, his financial status may eventually cause problems for him.

The missionary children may be deeply hurt because it seems that, due to their social standing and their parents' ministry, they cannot have any true friends. The poor children who desire their friendship may be looking for handouts or casing the house for possible opportunities to steal. It seems as though the missionary children have to make new friends every few months, as the familiar ones begin to beg, carry off items that are not nailed down, and generally take advantage of the gringo's kindness. The missionary is robbed by his "friends" because, in the past, he never had to question the honesty of his friends or neighbors. It is a matter of changing his way of thinking, which will result in a change in his lifestyle.

The missionary is not used to living behind locked doors and gates. He is not accustomed to hiding his belongings behind fortified walls. One of the first things new missionaries note in foreign countries is the high walls surrounding the homes. Americans are not used to this. They have been raised with the "open yard" policy. This carelessness is not permitted on the mission field.

The missionary leaves his garden hose in the front yard and parks his bicycle on the sidewalk during the day. His friends and neighbors may warn him, but it will take genuine effort on his part to be as careful as the nationals are.

Nationals are suspicious of everyone. That is why their walls are high and embedded with broken glass. Their metal fences have spears on the posts, and the German shepherd is mean. The nationals do not allow strangers to enter their homes. The missionary is not quite so paranoid; he is trying to be kind so he can win these strangers to Christ. This "open house" policy is commendable, but will be ridiculed by the nationals who have been robbed. The new missionary would do well to take the advice of experience.

Frequently, a relationship with someone poor will begin on a good note. The missionary's greatest desire is to see anyone come to Christ. For that reason, he is extremely friendly and can be taken advantage of very easily. After a period of time, just by the mere fact that many poor despise the rich, some will begin to despise the missionary. Although the poor enjoy using the missionary's equipment and car, they begin to disdain him because he is among the "haves" and they are among the "have-nots." This attitude may even be true of believers and national pastors.

I led my 80 year old neighbor lady to Christ but she would NEVER come into our home, even though I invited her many times. She said she was poor and I was rich and she knew her place.

There could be deep-rooted feelings about the significant salary disparity between the national pastor and the missionary. There may also be a real feeling of inequality as the national may think the missionary has never had to experience:

1. A hungry day in his life.

2. A lack of enough funds to buy food and the necessities of life.

3. An inflation rate of 100-500 percent annually.

4. Living in a mud hut with a dirt floor or in a slum area of town.

5. Making $1.25 an hour with prices equal to or higher than those in the United States.

6. The desire to tithe but the fear of not meeting daily needs.

7. The desire to send children to free public education, but having no funds for uniforms or materials.

8. The death of a child just because proper, simple medical help was not affordable.

Hindering Independence

A missionary is usually well-funded and well-equipped. His equipment and financial assistance may greatly help a struggling church, but they could also cause problems with indigenous principles. Dependence upon the missionary can stymie real church growth. How he uses his tithe could help or hinder his work.

The missionary may obtain a gift-loan for his church. A gift-loan consists of gifts from supporters that provide interest-free loans to churches on the mission field. This loan could mean the difference between a poor or middle-class building. Usually, this kind of loan is unavailable to a church that does not have a missionary as pastor. Lacking this opportunity could cause hard feelings, especially among those national pastors who are struggling with poor facilities.

Loaning Money or Equipment

Because a missionary has access to funds, he may become a prospective loan association. Both believers and unbelievers with sincere problems may want to borrow money. Their problems are so serious and long-standing that there seems to be no solution. This kind of situation tugs at the compassionate heart of the missionary.

Although a missionary may be sincere, he will not build a strong church or make lasting friends by loaning money to either the saved or the unsaved. Some will come to his church just for the handouts or the hope of such, even without encouraging gestures from the dedicated missionary/pastor. If the missionary is unwilling to lend money, he may appear hard or uninterested in the welfare of the poor. If he does loan money, he may encounter more serious problems. If he loans money:

1. He may never see it again.

2. When it is paid back, it may have only half its original value because of inflation and exchange rate differences.

3. The borrower may abandon the church because of an inability to repay. He has "lost face."

4. The borrower may begin to despise the missionary, being in debt to the "gringo."

5. The missionary may cause hard feelings if he discriminates in the choice of who borrows from him.

Because he has access to high-quality American products at low prices, the missionary may be asked to bring items back from the States. If he does, it may put him in embarrassing situations. He could even suffer financially when the item is refused due to a change of mind, a defect, or lack of funds. The refusal to follow through on the deal will provide the missionary with an involuntary means of unnecessarily increasing his equipment inventory.

Class Distinctions

Some poor will, at times, not desire to fellowship with the rich. This attitude may seem hard to understand, but it has been true for years. The lifestyles between the rich and the poor are totally different. Even their thinking patterns are in stark contrast.

If a middle-class or upper-class person entered a church of poorer-class people, he may receive a cold welcome. The same could happen if the situation were reversed. The missionary is one person who can bridge the gap between the rich and the poor. Even though he is welcome in the homes of both classes, he may never be able to create an atmosphere that will eliminate this long-standing, unbiblical social problem.

One can always reach down the social ladder, but rarely reach up. The poor will usually attend a middle-class or upper-class church. They may not stay long if they are not made to feel at home. It is a rare thing for the rich or middle-class to attend a poor church. One reason for this is that these poor churches have, by unfortunate necessity, been built in the poor areas of town.

Without the help of these better-financed national believers, even if only some are from the middle class, a church will always struggle. They may never be able to call a capable national pastor or reach the point where they can start other churches, both of which should be goals of the missionary/pastor.

Household Help

One thing that will really change in the new missionary's lifestyle is the need for a household servant. The missionary never had one in the States and probably did not even know anyone who did. His family and friends could not pay even minimum wage for help even if it was needed. The living conditions of most mission fields will almost demand household help. The missionary may have to:

1. Boil all water for twenty minutes and filter it.

2. Clean all vegetables with soap and chlorine.

3. Dust the whole house every day.

4. Do the laundry by hand due to a lack of water, electricity, or machines.

5. Teach the children, thus taking the regular time used for household care.

These needs will vary according to the extent of modern equipment available. Some live in conditions comparable to those in San Francisco or Dallas, while others may live in areas where electricity is uncommon and running water is unavailable.

Besides the daily care of the necessities of life, the missionary wife is also compelled to get involved in the work. This compulsion comes from the supporting churches or mission board, or perhaps her own compassion and calling. She may teach Sunday school, lead a ladies' group, go calling, teach the illiterate, instruct people in how to teach, or lead a children's or adult choir. All this is done because, in the early stages of the work, no one else is available to do it.

When money discussions arise someone is bound to ask why missionaries employ servants. Missionaries employ nationals for work women at home do it themselves for a variety of reasons. When a husband and wife go to the mission field the wife is justly and logically considered to be a missionary in her own right. The wife at home in no sense enters into the calling of her husband. On the mission field the wife of the missionary is a homemaker to be sure. But she is also a missionary and is supposed to engage in that activity. To do so means she must have help around the home to care for the necessary functions which require attention under any circumstances. She was not sent to the mission field to wash dishes and do laundry. She was sent to be a missionary. On most mission fields, it is cheaper for one to engage the services of a national to do household and other work than it is to do the work oneself. The cost of labor is so small when compared to the benefits reaped that it is not good business sense to be without this help. Servants have proved to be a necessity, not a luxury, and missionaries do not live like kings nor enjoy an easy life because they employ servants. (Lindsell, 1955, pp. 154-155)

Even though the missionary finds it necessary or helpful to have some servants, he would be doing himself a favor by:

1. Not hiring people in the church. It could cause very bad feelings. He could easily lose that person as a member, as well as anyone else the servant could convince.

2. Not paying excessively above the normal standard. If he does, he will only be hurting himself in future relationships with that servant. The missionary will be taken advantage of enough because of his ignorance or compassion; he does not need to invite it.

3. Not becoming familiar with the servants to the

extent that they become part of the family. This will only cause harder working relationships and may be the end of a good servant.

4. Having the wife deal with the women servants and the husband deal with the men servants. The man should never pay the woman servant nor become friendly with her in any way. His whole ministry may be in jeopardy if he violates this important rule.

5. Not leaving money or small, expensive items within easy access. There is no logical reason to tempt a person to be dishonest. Thievery has happened many times, and the servant is lost to you and to your Christian influence.

Concern for the Physically Needy

A missionary serving in a third-world country often experiences situations he has never encountered before. He may see incurable diseases that are new to him. He will see congenital disabilities that could have been treated and cured easily within the first few weeks or years of life. For the lack of funds or facilities, the person, who is now a teen or adult, is permanently crippled, cross-eyed, blind, or deaf. He may even encounter the dreadful disease of leprosy. This experience will eat at his heart. The missionary has deep compassion for the spiritual condition of the people to whom he ministers; this same feeling extends to their physical needs.

These pressing needs that catch the missionary's attention are not just about sickness but also about the everyday necessities of life. When a missionary sees the nationals in great need and suffering, his heart goes out to them. He is not a social worker, nor was he commissioned by Christ for such a ministry. He has been called, commissioned, and ordained to make disciples and start churches.

What can the missionary do? The needs are everywhere, and he is constantly reminded of the suffering around him, in stores, on the street, in the park, on the bus, in the church, and even at his front door. If the missionary is inexperienced enough to converse with those in need, his accent will cause the dollar signs to light up in the eyes of the hopeful.

It is true that some use even the slightest physical defect as an opportunity to earn a meager living without honest work. These can usually be noticed immediately. There are enough real cases of desperate need that the missionary will not have to go searching for them. There are more needy people than the missionary could hope to help in one hundred years. He must learn to steel himself against a recurring pattern of human need that he cannot possibly meet.

If one could stand by and watch the masses of people pass the beggars on the street, one could learn something. Most nationals pay no attention to the crying needs of their own people. The ones that do help usually do so with a desperate hope of taking time off their sentence in purgatory, or alleviating the suffering for themselves or another one in purgatory.

There are a few national government programs available like those in the United States. There are no unemployment benefits or welfare handouts, and few charity organizations. If any help is available, it is usually channeled through a church that teaches salvation by works.

When the missionary realizes that he has so much in terms of health and material possessions compared to his fellow Christians or nationals, he has a great desire to share or help. Still, he does not want people to begin to depend on him. The result of this dependency would not be conducive to building a strong, self-supporting church.

Helping nationals without causing dependency is not easy, but perhaps the "Missionary Under Commission" chart below will more easily clarify the situation:

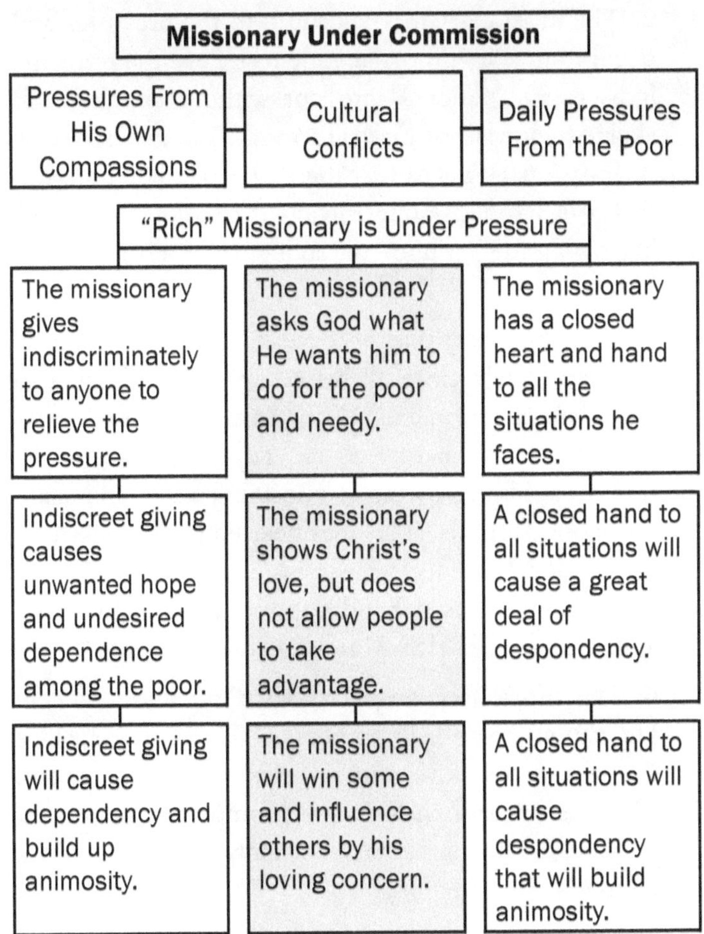

1. The missionary is under pressure from his own compassion and the requests of the poor, both saved and unsaved. "He is the rich American missionary, the man who has more than he needs, the one God could use to ease my burden if he would just open up and start sharing what he has," think some nationals.

2. The missionary may succumb to the pressures and begin to give to almost anyone to relieve the pressure, indiscreetly. Nationals are not without cunning and skill in their ways of making appeals. The generosity of the missionary will cause others to depend on him, and this usually builds animosity, as the national does not like owing the "gringo" or having to be subservient to him.

3. The missionary may become extremely hardhearted and completely close all his compassion, refusing to even listen to problems. If the missionary establishes this pattern of hardness, he may even have rocks thrown at his car by those who think he should share his "good fortune." This hardhearted policy will cause despondency among those in his church who have real needs. This "closed hand" approach will also build animosity as the "rich American" does not care.

4. The missionary ought to ask God if and where He wants him to help someone. This method can be a way to show love and concern for others' needs. The missionary's charity may prompt a few spiritual decisions. The missionary certainly will not build a church by this method.

Financing The Church Work

Monetary problems are not among the most popular subjects. Christ spent more time preaching on money and its related problems than on any other subject. Brazil's avrage monthly salary is $320, in other countries, it is much less. This critical financial situation has persisted for centuries and caused many serious problems. The purpose of this section is to explore how a missionary can build a self-supporting, self-governing, and self-propagating church with the tithes of the poor and middle classes.

Tithing

Without being legalistic, the missionary must teach tithing to his believers and new converts. Every believer who wants to please the Lord must tithe. However, it is more difficult to tithe when one is poor. Just because each believer tithes 10% equally, the results are not equal. Consider a man who earns $60 a month (minimum salary in Cuba) and another who earns $1,000 a month. One can live much more easily on $900 a month than on $54, especially when both parties pay the same for food, clothing, and shelter.

The only way to correctly judge one's ability to buy or tithe is to work on the day's-wages scale. A day's wages is how much money a person can make in one day, and the scale is how much buying power that money has.

The following prices are based on the minimum wages in Brazil and the United States, adjusted to 2026. If an American had to spend the same percentage of his wages to buy the following items in Brazil, this is what he would have to pay:

Gas .... *$27 per gallon*

Oil .... *$69 per quart*

Eggs .... *$8 per dozen*

Milk .... *$42 per gallon*

Hamburger .... *$15 per pound*

A bicycle .... *$1,300 for a simple one*

An iPhone 17 .... *$9,600*

When the national tithes, the missionary must rejoice with him and trust the Lord to bless him, proving His faithfulness. It is not hard to see how difficult it would be to tithe under these circumstances.

The missionary is not a social worker, but caring for people is part of the gospel. Faith without works is dead. The missionary can try to help by finding jobs, housing, medical care, food, and clothing. These things must be done carefully so as not to attract or create "rice Christians." The term "rice Christians" originated with missionaries in the Orient, referring to professing believers who came to the church to obtain rice and appeared interested in the message. It is especially easy to attract these, and hard for the new missionary to recognize when it is happening.

Building Projects

It has been estimated that a church needs about one hundred in attendance to have sufficient funds to support a national pastor and church buildings. There are only a few church buildings that are adequate for one hundred people. The problem is obvious. How can a small, struggling group, just beginning, finance a building that will seat 100 people to meet their future needs, without wasting their present funds on an inadequate building?

Another aspect to consider is that the building must be sufficient to meet the needs of the continually rising middle class. Without attracting the middle class, a work will always be weak and unable to support itself properly or reach out to help others. It will also lack the capable leadership that it will need in the future.

The missionary's goal is to build churches strong enough to start other churches. Churches need to be built strong enough to carry some of the financial and leadership load of the schools and camps. How can these churches be financed?

1. To save money and build as you go is a poor method. In most countries, inflation is so high that it is impossible to keep up with the price of building materials.

2. Could the church borrow the money from a national bank? Most churches built in the United States use this method because interest rates are very low and inflation is almost nonexistent. But in most third-world countries, it would be impossible; the church cannot meet the demands of both the high interest rates and soaring inflation.

3. The missionary could build the church completely with United States funds, but it would always be the "gringo's" church. This dependent method would not promote the indigenous policy.

4. The church may borrow the money from the missionary at no interest. This is usually called a "gift loan." It should be paid back in dollars, or the missionary will not have any funds to repeat the same; the inflated exchange rate would eat them up. The only disadvantage of this method is that it could cause hard feelings when national believers have to repay it.

5. A more valuable way to build a stable church would be the "lot-bank" program. A group of believers is given a lot, and perhaps a building. The missionary or the mission agency donates this. Within a specified time, they must buy a lot of equal value, well-located for starting another church, and construct a building equal to their own. This method uses indigenous thinking and is a good plan. This method is explained in more detail in Chapter Five.

Reconciling Monetary Differences

The following are suggestions on how the missionary

can help the nationals without causing dependence on him or his mission agency, as well as precautions to follow for a successful, long-term ministry.

Helping Suggestions

1. At times, a missionary will see a need that he might provide through a one-time gift or by giving something that he already has. He may give clothes, dishes, tools, medicine, transportation, books, a bicycle, toys, or food. Birthdays are good opportunities to give without drawing attention.

2. If someone in the church is unemployed, it is possible to provide some work for them. If they work for the church, the church should pay them. If they work for the missionary, the missionary should pay them.

3. If someone in the church builds a home or tries to improve his living conditions, the missionary may help or hire someone to work in his place.

4. On occasions, the missionary will find opportunities to help in the civil area. In Brazil, it costs half a month's wages to get married civilly. Some of the new converts will not be married legally. If the missionary could secure contributions for this legal matter, he could help these couples qualify for recommendation for church membership.

5. A simple Bible will cost about one day's wages. If the missionary could obtain gifts for this fund, he could buy the Bibles and sell them to the believers at a fifty percent discount.

6. If members of the church have great needs, these needs should be brought to the attention of the deacons. The church should help one time, but if the needy member has a job and will not tithe to the church,

then further help should not be extended. How could the church encourage people to disobey God?

Precautions

1. Do not advertise giveaway items in the church. People will be knocking each other down in the rush. If you give away candy at Christmas, do not tell anyone until after the program.

2. Do not give money to beggars. They will most likely spend it on cigarettes or liquor. If one wants to help, they can give food and the gospel. Many of the children who will really get to your heart are trained beggars, providing for a drunken father.

3. Care must be taken so that the missionary does not appear to be bragging about his financial status or exhibiting it for awe. The poor will quickly notice it and despise this kind of attitude. At the same time, hiding it or denying it does not work, as the American missionary is expected to be "rich."

4. Although it would be easy to do, the missionary must be careful not to show partiality toward the upper class. This problem is not new. Christ and James both mentioned it (*James 2:4-6*). It happens because the missionary wants some friends on his own economic level. He eagerly desires to win a person to Christ who could financially help the work reach self-supporting status much sooner.

5. If the missionary finds that he cannot adjust to ministering among the poor, then he may have to change his area of work. The middle or upper class needs a witness. There are many modern cities in foreign countries where the lifestyle may not be much different than that in the United States.

Conclusion

Life experiences have proven that one does not make friends by giving away money or items. Confusion, distrust, dependency, and even hatred may result. America's foreign policies over the last 100 years should prove that. Yet there are ways to help, and the compassionate missionary will feel compelled to do so.

The missionary cannot be the big brother to all who need help. If he even tried, he would soon dissipate all his funds, for there will always be a need. The way he handles this problem may mean the difference between an indigenous church and an American relief station.

Lay not up for yourselves treasures upon earth, where moth and rust doth corrupt, and where thieves break through and steal: But lay up for yourselves treasures in heaven, where neither moth nor rust doth corrupt, and where thieves do not break through nor steal: For where your treasure is, there will your heart be also.

Matthew 6:19-21

CHAPTER 4
Evangelism on the Foreign Field

Introduction - Divine Command

The Great Commission is not an option; it is God's command for every believer. It was not given just to the apostles. The commands to evangelize the world are: *Matthew 28:18-20*, *Mark 16:15*, *Luke 24:47-48*, *John 20:21*, and *Acts 1:8*. The chief command with the most information is also the most popular text concerning the program of God for this dispensation. *Matthew 28:18-20* is a text dealing with winning souls, discipling, and teaching the whole counsel of the Word of God.

Aggressive world evangelism was a new idea when Christ gave it. Christ presented His "Magna Carta" of missionary endeavor with a declaration of His power over all heaven and earth. The word "power" is "exousia," which means "authority." Christ had been given all the divine authority to mount a Christian Army.

The plan of *Matthew 28:18-20* came with a promise. The promise being that Christ would be with the one witnessing even unto the end of the age. The plan was simple: go, teach (make disciples), baptize, and teach all the Word of God, trusting the promise of His presence.

The will of God for every believer is to bring others to the Savior. Evangelism is from the heart of God, the center of the Old Testament, and the "heartbeat" of the church in the New Testament era.

> *World evangelism is no afterthought on the part of God. It is not an emergency plan, nor is it a sudden scheme devised by God due to the alteration of some previous purpose. The missionary enterprise in the New Testament pours forth like a great river. Its headwaters flow from Old Testament revelation.* (Lewis, 1962, p. 20)

Prerequisite To Evangelism

1. A knowledge of the people is necessary, which would include customs and culture. *Custom, utterly foreign to the missionary and seemingly without any consistency, when interpreted correctly, makes missionaries blush with shame as they learn from the nationals they have come to teach. But it is safe to say no missionary can be a good evangelist who does not comprehend the customs of the people. The failure to do so results in embarrassments and dislocations which make ineffectual the endeavors of the most zealous missionaries.* (Lindsell, 1965, p. 192)

2. It is necessary to know something of the major religious system of the country. One of the basic "laws of teaching" is to take the pupil from the known to the unknown. There are examples of this teaching method in the New Testament. Christ brought new truths to the scholarly Jew through Old Testament examples. The sacrificial lamb of the Old Testament was the Lamb of God in the Person of Christ (*John 1:29*). As Moses lifted the serpent in the desert, so was Christ to be lifted on the cross (*John 3:14*). God gave the Israelites manna from heaven to satisfy their physical hunger. Christ was the Bread of Life to satisfy the hunger of the Jews of His day (*John 6*). Jacob's well provided water for thirsty bodies, and Christ was the Living Water for thirsty souls (*John 4*).

3. An understanding of the national's thinking patterns is necessary. Understanding the national is not easy; he is a complete enigma to the new missionary. *An understanding of the mind is another prerequisite to effective evangelism. By the mind of the people is meant their thought patterns, the way they themselves reason and react to life in its multiform relationships. Outward actions may be identical, but the mind behind the thought may differ greatly. Thus, two people coming from different backgrounds may do the same thing but to each the act may have connotations which vary and may arise from a mind set that bears no relationship one to the other.* (Lindsell, 1965, p. 193)

4. The missionary needs more than a surface knowledge of the Scriptures to defend any part of his faith and to explain any false doctrine in the light of the Word of God.

5. The missionary needs a good control of the language, more than just a novice level. He should never quit learning the language, for there will always be new idioms to pick up. When he thinks he is at a good conversational level, he encounters a professor or politician who leaves him in the dark with a score of new vocabulary terms.

6. Effective evangelism requires a comprehensive outreach to all classes and all people everywhere. A missionary is a soulwinner wherever he goes.

7. A personal one-on-one relationship is necessary for effective evangelism. This will be his list of prospects, which will never leave him without possible contacts. Understanding the people is of first importance. One must take them from where they find them to where God wants them spiritually. The missionary will find few people coming to Christ without problems in their lives. These people are ripe for a lifestyle change and

are looking for an answer to burdensome problems.

The dedicated missionary is in a strong position to understand a primitive people because, though he is an observer, he is more than an observer. He really cares about the people! The highest praise the local people often give to the missionaries is the sentence, "They have loved us." (Trueblood, 1972, p. 13)

The Ultimate Goal of Evangelism

The gospel is to be carried to the ends of the earth. That is the command given almost 2,000 years ago. The apostles did their best to carry the message to the known world. If Paul ever got to Spain as he desired (*Romans 15:24, 28*), then he went as far west as he could.

It is to the credit of the church that she continually sought to cross new frontiers and to assail fresh barriers. Her penetration of jungles and tribes, the crossing of deserts and mountains, the reduction of hundreds of languages into writing, have all been commendable and heroic. (Fife, 1978, p. 184)

There should be only one clear-cut goal to all this suffering and trial: evangelism—the establishment of local, independent, indigenous churches. Church planting was the goal of the apostles and the fulfillment of Christ's promise (*Matthew 16:18*) and command (*Matthew 28:18-20*). All other agencies or outreaches must come under the auspices, support, and control of the local church. Every missionary should be a church planter in one way or another. One is sadly mistaken if he thinks that he can relegate the establishment of churches to the periphery of the goals chart.

The result of evangelism is to reproduce oneself. The reproduction will not be complete until the new convert is himself winning souls. The chain must not be broken.

Every Christian is encouraged to participate in one way or another and feel not only that he belongs to the group, but that he is needed by the group. As soon as a person becomes a Christian, he is expected to begin witnessing and, soon after, to start a Sunday school class (or Bible study) in his home. This method encourages the fullest utilization of every member of the church. (Fife, 1978, p. 186)

The Message of the Missionary

An Ambassador For Christ

Every missionary is an ambassador for Christ (*II Corinthians 5:20*). An ambassador has some very unique responsibilities:

1. He is the official representative for a king or government.

2. He has no original message; he can only transmit the exact message from the sender.

3. He attempts to promote well-being between the people and the party he is representing.

The missionary is not an ambassador for his home country. He is not called to promote his culture or governmental system. He is to promote the King of Kings through the message of the cross of Calvary.

The Lord's ambassador has a message no earthly ambassador has the privilege of proclaiming. He is not reconciling men to men, although this is a clear and positive result of his ministry. He is to reconcile men to God, through Christ, the only mediator between God and men.

The missionary's message is clear. He is not an ambassador of goodwill, but of "good news." He can only imitate the message of the cross, duplicating the apostles' work.

"We are sent," in the words of Hugh Thomas Kerr, "not to preach sociology but salvation; not economics but evangelism; not reform but redemption; not culture but conversion; not progress but pardon; not the new social order but the new birth; not revolution but regeneration; not renovation but revival; not resuscitation but resurrection; not a new organization but a new creation; not democracy but the gospel; not civilization but Christ. We are the ambassadors (of Christ) not diplomats." (Zwemer, 1976, pp. 37-38)

A Compassionate Invitation

The message involves a great deal more than just telling the story. It also includes the compassion and tears of the messenger. Salvation is simple and easy because Someone else paid the terrible price. To make salvation just a matter of repeating a printed prayer would be to fall into the meaningless rituals of religion. Religion is man reaching up to God with a handful of good works, hoping that God will look with favor upon the possibility that his good works outweigh his sins. Christianity is God reaching down through the nail-scarred hands of Christ, offering. salvation freely.

There are only two things necessary for salvation: repentance from sin and reception of Christ as the only and all-sufficient Savior. It is easy to complicate this simple message with a list of rules. The list of rules is given to save the sinner or to guarantee the salvation of the believer. There will be plenty of this type of legalism for the missionary to battle. It will give his work more trouble than persecution. If the missionary falls into the unfortunate trap of expecting a reformation before salvation, he is practicing the same error to which the Galatians fell prey. It is salvation first by repentance and the new birth. Then, and only then, can the new convert have victory over the sin in his life.

The Methods of the Missionary

The type of evangelism used on any field, or in any specific area of that field, will be determined by the types of people living there and the extent of their exposure to the gospel. There are many methods of evangelism.

Whatever method is used, it must result in the salvation of souls and the establishing of local churches. The social approach to missions is not found in the Bible. Paul's purpose was to preach the gospel and start churches. He did not feel obligated nor led by the Lord to fight slavery or improve health and living conditions (*I Corinthians 2:2*).

The missionary may use methods of work other than preaching. Each method, whether it be medical help, teaching English, or operating a Christian bookstore, must have evangelism as its primary goal. All branches of outreach should be under the auspices and control of the local churches in that area, or the work can easily slide into a neo-evangelical position.

Methods must accomplish goals; otherwise, they have no reason to be used. They will be just spinning wheels and noise without harmony.

Missions involves the proper balance between message and methods. Theology deals with content of the message. Methodology delineates the means of communication. Theology without methodology leads to complacency devoid of compassion for the lost, methodology without accompanying theology divests the gospel of its power, reducing missions to a high pressured human enterprise. (Amstutz, N.D., p. 55)

Methods that are outside the realm of the direction and the power of the Holy Spirit must be put aside. The Holy Spirit could never lead anyone to do anything that would contradict the Word of God. The missionary depends on the Holy Spirit to guide him and bring him to the curious and the seeking. But alas, this leading is sometimes hindered by the failure to keep the fires burning between the missionary and the Holy Spirit. The natural tendency of any fire is to go out, no matter what size it is. The natural tendency is for the glow and fervor of the missionary's heart to dissipate. He needs to keep the bellows going to feed the fire of his compassion.

City Work

Paul spent his time in the major cities of his day. He must have had the idea of planting churches in the major population areas. The gospel would then be carried from there to the interior cities by the transitory believers. In the first century, some believers were scattered abroad by persecution (*I Thessalonians 1:8*). Their faith had been spread abroad, so that the Apostles did not have to preach or teach anything.

Many times, the pattern of starting in the major cities is not followed by modern-day missionaries. It is easier to construct a church in the interior towns, where land is cheaper, and living expenses are lower. But fewer people live in the interior, and they are more steeped in the national religion and traditions, making them harder to reach.

> *The failure of the church, then is basically threefold. First, she has failed to keep those members who have migrated from the country to the city. Secondly, she has failed to make an impression on the city masses with the gospel. Thirdly, she has failed to produce the kind of city church with a missionary heart that reaches out to evangelize the surrounding rural area.* (Fife, 1978, p.183)

There are good reasons why the cities must be evangelized first. They must be evangelized first because:

1. It is the biblical way to do it.

2. They are the center of government control. Although the missionary is not involved in politics, politics will determine the extent of his religious freedom and permission to stay in the country.

3. They are the centers of education. No class is wooed more assiduously by the communists than students. The communists have been all too successful in their advance through this method.

4. They have the middle and upper classes that can provide funds and leadership to a central force reaching into the interior.

5. City people are easier to reach because of their disruptive lifestyle. They have already uprooted their family ties, so it will not be quite so hard to get them to change their religion.

6. They are the communication centers that feed the interior with newspapers, radio, and TV.

For some, the challenge of working in cities may represent the acid test of their obedience as well as of imagination. Many of the world's cities are ugly, sordid places and few would chose to live and work there out of any natural desire. But we dare not flinch in the face of this enormous task, for at stake are huge possibilities, both for success and failure. If we lose the cities we lose the world. (Fife, 1978, p.260)

Total Discipleship Program

The chart on the next page is given to formulate a clearer view of the total discipleship program. A tape recorder can give the message, but only a person can make disciples in the biblical sense of the word. Discipling is basically just reproducing oneself spiritually. If this program is followed, the missionary will probably retain about 80% of his converts.

Total Discipleship Chart

Contact and Curious	A. Initial Contact	Street, Park, Bus Store, Neighborhood
	B. Planned Meeting	Social Empnhasis Spiritual Emphasis
	C. Interest Stirred	Theological Questions Answering Problems
Conviction and Conversion	A. Give Invitation	Reject Good Works Salvation by Grace
	B. Accept Christ	Repentance from Sin Faith Toward God
	C. Train Disciples	New Convert Classes Home Bible Studies
Confirmation and Continuance	A. Give Guidance	Spiritual Example Alternate Activities
	B. Stress Evangelism	Accompanies Another Solo Experience
	C. Active Member	Church Leadership A Pastoral Call

Contacts and Curious

The missionary should be on alert for Initial Contacts, especially those God brings across his path; these always seem to be His best converts. The use of good, attractive literature is indispensable to the growth of any work. The value of literature distribution is evident in the communist production and use of literature.

The communists produce annually at least three pieces of literature for every man, woman, and child on the face of the earth. It has been a significant factor in their conquest of over one-third of the world's total population. And yet according to the French communist newspaper, Peace and Liberty, "The gospel is a much more powerful weapon for the renewal of society than our Marxist philosophy." We might add that the gospel can do much more than renew society. (Fife, 1978, p.210)

The advantages of using literature can be seen in that: once it is mass produced, the initial work is done; it can speak clearly, directly, and without negative impressions or accents created by a foreign tongue and face; it can work twenty-four hours, week in and week out, conveying its message without becoming jaded or lukewarm; it can be screened against "foreigners" and can proclaim its message within the context of the culture. (Fife, 1978, pp. 218-220)

If the missionary spends much time on the bus, he can use that time to witness and hand out literature. This cannot be done on a large scale. It must be kept personal, or the "foreigner" might be thrown off the bus.

In local stores, the missionary could make friends with the owners and workers. Repeated invitations to the church and to Bible study could open doors. Giving tracts and returning to find out what was learned is a very good way to open the door to "friendship evangelism."

Passing out tracts on the street will not be very profitable unless it is done in the church's neighborhood. Local parks and amusement centers are excellent places to distribute tracts and make contacts with teens.

The missionary may have an opportunity to answer the question, "What is the difference between the Catholic church and the Baptist church?" This opportunity should not be taken as a chance to criticize the Catholic church. It is a great opportunity to explain that salvation is by grace alone, something their church violently opposes.

People are slow to accept foreigners with a new religion. They have been lied to and deceived by cult groups for years. They have been mistreated by these groups, which are more interested in selling their literature or destroying coffee pots than they are in the destiny of eternal souls.

From the initial contacts nationals can be invited to Planned Meetings. These meetings can be in the church or in the missionary's home. Sometimes the national invites the missionary to his home. This type of invitation is usually only given by the upper class. The missionary should pray for an opportunity to bring up the subject of salvation or "religion" in the conversation. If it isn't, then the subject should not be pushed at this early stage of contact, for the national will resent it and nothing will be accomplished.

With no need to study and only spending a few hours a week, one can make good contacts via an English class. The missionary should limit these lessons to the middle or upper classes, as his goal is to open doors to evangelism, not to teach English.

Social emphasis can be placed on activities, but the missionary's goal should not be forgotten. He may plan youth sporting events to reach many interested unsaved teens, but the aim of evangelism must remain. The activities should not be just for the sake of entertainment. The biggest problems occur when 60% or more of the attendees are unsaved. It is difficult to control that kind of atmosphere, and it would be better to limit the group's size and manage it more closely.

Street meetings are still an acceptable method of preaching the gospel. They are more easily accepted among the lower class and in rural areas. Care must be taken to ensure that the charismatics don't take over the meeting, that no one else is handing out literature from their group, and that the crowd is under control at all times.

Evangelistic meetings in the churches are profitable when held from Friday through Sunday. These meetings are a good opportunity to have a national speaker. Advertising seems to do very little to bring new people to the meetings. Most visitors will be members' friends and will have been invited many times.

House-to-house evangelism is not very productive.

Actually, *Acts 20:20* does not refer to "cold turkey" house-to-house calling. Paul taught the Word of God in many homes that were open to him. This type of evangelism could only have a meaningful result if it advertised the church and gave its location.

One of the best ways to get into new homes is to hold a Bible study in a believer's home. He invites his neighbors, and then the same kind of study could be repeated in their home.

Activities with a spiritual emphasis, such as a ladies' tea, a men's breakfast, a birthday party, a celebration of national holidays, etc., are great opportunities to introduce unsaved people to church people. Many would attend activities like these, because they would have no fear of being undesirably indoctrinated.

Meetings for children can be held in the church or in a believer's home. Puppets will always help draw children and retain their interest. For salvation, each child must be addressed individually. They have been drilled since babyhood into repeating prayers; therefore, they must understand that a prayer to receive Christ as Savior is not just another good work that helps them save themselves. It is usually wise not to baptize children until they are teens, unless their parents are members of the church. Unless their parents are reached, many children and teens disappear into the worldly system. A missionary will not build a truly indigenous church by doing most of his work among children or teens.

The missionary wants the national's interest stirred. People may have questions about theological subjects. They usually ask something like this, "Is it true that if a person smokes, he cannot be saved or will lose his salvation?" or "Can a lady cut her hair and still be saved?" Some questions may be deeper theologically than these.

The missionary can also stir up interest by asking some of his own questions, such as, "If I could show you five verses in the Bible where God says that good works cannot save, would you believe it?" The Apostle Paul used this method in Athens, where he answered the three greatest questions of life. (*Acts 17:22-34*)

The missionary has the answers to life's greatest questions:

1. How did I get here?

2. Why am I here?

3. Where am I going after this life?

The missionary also has solutions for the way out of the mud of sin and hopelessness. People with problems are easy prey for the cult groups, which usually give a list of rules for salvation. The people in the "gutter" of life are ready for any system that will deliver them from their chains of bondage. It is easy for them to accept the way of reformation rather than regeneration. They have to make such a little change from the old system (usually Catholic), they move from one list of rules to another, without a real born-again experience.

The missionary will find himself involved in counseling sessions to address some of these life problems. Although the only counseling the missionary can do must come from the Bible, he also must consider the cultural setting.

> *Anthropologists have tended to focus upon man and culture while neglecting the individual. Psychologists have tended to focus on individuals to the neglect of cultural consideration. Some missionaries tend to focus on eternal values of the redeemed and neglect both the individual needs and cultural considerations.* (Hasselgrave, 1984, p. 148)

The missionary must give the answers that God has already given. This is called "Nouthetic Counseling." It is described more specifically in Jay Adams' many books on counseling. If the person will not come to Christ, he has no spiritual power, no matter how many lists of rules he keeps or how positive he thinks he is! (Adams, 1970, N.P.)

Some basic principles to follow when counseling are:

1. A clear definition of the problem in concrete terms is needed from the beginning.

2. There needs to be an investigation of the solutions attempted so far.

3. There needs to be a clear definition of the change to be achieved.

4. There needs to be a plan formulated and implemented to produce change. (Hasselgrave, 1984, p.33)

Conviction And Conversion

The missionary must do more than preach; he must give invitations. Before the missionary can invite the national to accept Christ, he must be sure the unsaved person understands that salvation is entirely by the grace of God. This is not easily accomplished and will probably not be understood at the first encounter. The United States has had preaching on the Grace of God for over 200 years, whereas most of the mission fields have had a system of good works for salvation for over 400 years. It will be hard to break that barrier, but thank God it is not the missionary's job to do so. It is the job of the Holy Spirit through the preaching and teaching of the missionary.

It is not enough to quote a list of verses to a Catholic and ask him to pray a certain prayer. They were raised on repetitive prayers, and praying with you, a religious leader, would be even better. They repeat the prayer, and the missionary may rejoice that they have been saved. But perhaps no name was actually written in the Lamb's Book of Life because there was never really a clear rejection of good works. The Holy Spirit did not have time to convict of sin and convince the lost one of salvation by grace alone. Giving the lost time to think things through is an important part of true discipling.

If an invitation is given after every meeting, it is not always wise to ask those who want to respond to come forward. This type of invitation is strange to them, and some may even come to have a show of spirituality. It is well to encounter each one at the door, to ask whether they have any needs or would like to accept Christ, and to try to schedule appointments to visit them at home.

Repentance of sin is necessary for biblical acceptance of Christ. True repentance should not be confused with reformation. Biblical repentance means a change of mind which, with the power of the Holy Spirit, will result in a change of life (*I Corinthians 5:17*). The national must change his mind about:

1. <u>Christ's divinity</u>. Christ must be accepted as the divine, eternal Son of God, or one cannot be saved. All idolatry must be forsaken, and all the saints must be renounced.

2. <u>Salvation by good works</u>. This thought must be totally rejected. Many verses teach salvation by grace alone (*Isaiah 55:1-2; Isaiah 64:6; Ephesians 2:8-9; Romans 6:23; Titus 3:5; II Timothy 1:9;* and *Revelation 22:17*). If the national does not understand this, he cannot be saved. If someone believes they can lose their salvation, then they actually do believe in salvation by good works.

3. <u>Christ's Lordship</u>. Christ must be the Lord of the national's life. It is not just a matter of "trying Christ." The national cannot just experiment with the Savior to see if His way is better than any other way. His way is not better than any other way. His way is the only way.

Faith can be defined as confidence in the promises of God (*Romans 4:21*). The missionary's duty is to direct the national to place his faith in Christ—nothing else. It is the object of the national's faith that saves him, not the amount of faith he has (*Matthew 17:20-21*).

The missionary must train disciples. A baptismal class can be offered so the new covert can see that it is symbolic rather than a part of salvation, and then be baptized. Then, the rest of the new convert classes can be given. This will give the church time to see if the prospective church member is really serious about following Christ.

Having Bible studies in the nationals' homes will open doors for new contacts. Relatives and friends are always dropping by. The missionary can train some of his church members to handle this part of the program, thereby freeing him. The missionary can teach the leaders a lesson and send them out to teach the same lesson to others in the neighborhood. A group of five to ten is ideal.

Classes can also be given during the Sunday school hour or at a special training session on Wednesday or Sunday night. Having it on Sunday morning will provide an opportunity to form a habit of attending the Sunday school hour.

Confirmation and Continuance

The missionary must give guidance to the new convert. Guidance does not mean handing them a list of spiritual rules. Assigning another believer to be a spiritual "big brother" to the new convert—this is the way to direct the young Christian down the right path.

Church activities will give the new converts alternate options to replace the worldly ones they should drop. The missionary should not just change minds; he should also teach the nationals how to change their lifestyles.

The missionary must emphasize evangelism. The new convert should be encouraged to bring his friends and relatives to church. This new convert needs to be taught how to lead others to Christ. Someone must walk alongside the new convert until he learns to work on his own.

The missionary is trying to make the new convert an active member of the church. An active member attends even when it is not convenient and tithes even though it is a sacrifice. The missionary is trying to cultivate church leadership. He must allow these nationals to do something themselves; otherwise, they will never learn. Therefore, he cannot insist on doing all the work himself. If the missionary continues to do all the work himself, he will not build a strong church with capable leadership; he will only wear himself out, into an early retirement.

The final and glorious stage of evangelism will be when the Lord calls someone, possibly from that very congregation, into the ministry. This result would bring a great sense of achievement to the hard-working and well-organized missionary.

Evangelism Chart

The "Command of God to Evangelize" chart on the next page will help clarify the results of missionary work. To some, the missionary's soul-winning efforts seem to be a measure of his success as a servant of God. Other missionaries, the home office, agency, or supporting churches can apply pressure that causes some missionaries to go ahead of the Holy Spirit in winning souls. Of course, the missionary also wants to write interesting prayer letters so that the level of support will remain high and prayer for his ministry will not be lacking.

The previously mentioned pressures may lead the missionary to use unbiblical methods. He may find "converts" even where the Holy Spirit cannot. The

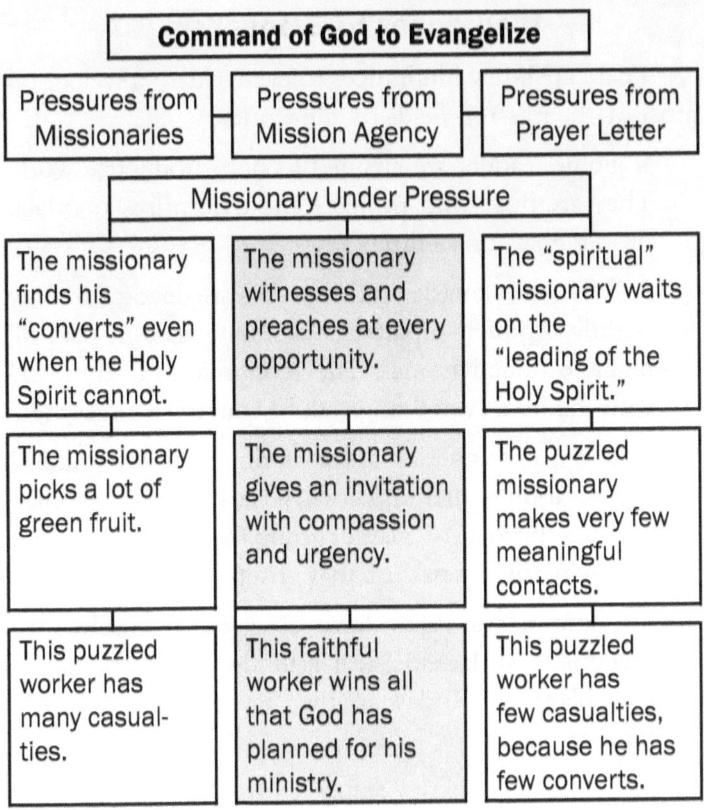

missionary is actually picking "green fruit" that may never ripen. He has many casualties, as these people were never converted, only convinced. The loss rate is high.

At the other end of the pendulum, the missionary may "wait" on the leading of the Lord. Therefore, he makes few plans and takes few steps toward evangelism. He has few casualties because he has few contacts and few converts.

God's will is that the missionary plans his efforts, witnessing and preaching at every opportunity. These plans could involve many facets of the previously mentioned program. These plans also involve giving an invitation with compassion and urgency. He will win all that the Lord planned.

Hindrances to Evangelism

There are a few hindrances to evangelism prevalent on most of the mission fields of the world:

1. Some leaders are chained to non-productive work. They are busy with projects and enterprises that lack proper goals or methods.

2. Some missionaries and churches are devoted to only slightly productive patterns of evangelism instead of highly productive ones. They continue to deal mostly with children, even though adults could also be reached.

3. Some missionaries are suffering under a political organization in their missionary agency, which requires a voting approval of a larger group for the advancement of any particular part of that group.

4. Some missionaries have resigned themselves to accepting the lackadaisical attitude about organizing and planning. Today is the day to organize, not tomorrow.

5. Some missionaries refuse to try anything that has not been previously used.

6. Some missionaries are not walking in the Spirit. They bicker and fuss among themselves, hindering the work and quenching the Holy Spirit's power.

Conclusion

Evangelism began with God's compassion. Its message was provided through the cross of Christ. Its power comes through the convicting work of the Holy Spirit. All of this divine help will be available to the missionary who walks in the Spirit and follows the Word of God.

Evangelism is the only reason for missions. Without evangelism, missions is only a religious peace corps. The sacrifices missionaries make are without meaning if evangelism is not the goal.

Church planting is the ultimate goal of evangelism. The Lord Jesus Christ gave the command to plant churches. The example of church planting comes from the apostles. The pattern for church planting comes from the Epistles. Without church planting, missions is a non-defined religious effort. The sacrifices the supporting churches make are not honored if local evangelistic churches are not built.

And he said unto them, It is not for you to know the times or the seasons, which the Father hath put in his own power. But ye shall receive power, after that the Holy Ghost is come upon you: and ye shall be witnesses unto me both in Jerusalem, and in all Judaea, and in Samaria, and unto the uttermost part of the earth.

Acts 1: 7-8

Dr. Latham's third church in Cachoeirinha, Rio Grande do Sul Brazil.

CACHOEIRINHA CITY COAT OF ARMS

CHAPTER 5
Releasing Churches
to the Nationals

Introduction - Prevailing Philosophies

Just how and when to turn the church over to the nationals has been a hotly debated issue. The goal of any biblical mission agency should be to establish churches and ensure that qualified national personnel lead them. This target may be harder to hit than the surface conditions indicate, and it may be approached from more ways than first realized.

In the past, both churches and pastors have been lost because either the church or the pastor, or perhaps both, were not prepared to meet the unexpected. Perhaps this was because of:

1. Disorganized administrative procedures.

2. Disgruntled missionary personnel.

3. Unprepared national personnel and church properties.

4. Undefined goals and procedures.

It could be a combination of all of the above. The purpose of this chapter will be to discuss the needs in all the above-mentioned areas except the second. The topic of disgruntled missionary personnel has already been discussed in Chapter Two.

When a missionary goes home on furlough, it is always better if he can say, "I started an indigenous church" or churches. It looks good on paper, but the true financial and spiritual condition of that work may never be known by the supporters, even if the work closes.

The following scenario seems to be a recurring pattern worldwide. The missionary has a small but dedicated group. He is anxious to start a church in his first term of missionary service. He is going home, and the pressure is on. He needs a good story and exciting slides to show. As soon as the missionary feels that the situation is right, he calls a young, ambitious man. This young preacher, who may also have a small family, is overjoyed to finally be in the ministry. He is willing to sacrifice to demonstrate his dedication. The fanfare is accomplished, and the church is handed over to the dedicated national pastor.

This pattern usually follows a single prevailing philosophy, which has proven disastrous in some cases. The philosophy is: with a few men, some women, and many children, the church is turned over to the nationals. His salary is established at the national minimum, which in Brazil, is $320-480 a month. This news sounds good in a prayer letter: "Successful Missionary Turns His Church Over to the Nationals." Now the missionary can go home on furlough, a veteran and an obvious success.

The Crisis in the Work

Behold, six months after the missionary goes home on furlough, the situation with the national church and pastor has changed drastically:

1. The pastor had to get a secular job to pay the bills because his wife had another child.

2. One male member moved to another town, leaving only three families and a group of children in the church.

3. Drought has struck, and many are out of work.

Everyone is in desperate straits. Tithes are down, and the pastor's salary is behind.

4. Everyone is discouraging each other and complaining, blaming the new pastor, because he is not quite what they expected. He is not nearly as well-funded or equipped as the missionary.

5. The pastor senses his delicate situation and leaves the ministry for more permanent and profitable work. He wants to provide for his family and not have the heartache and headache of leading a group of discontented people.

6. Upon hearing the sad news about his church on the field, the missionary comes to some "very logical" conclusions:

> a. the church was very excited and in good shape when I left for furlough;

> b. the national brethren have failed us again, not being willing to sacrifice when the going got tough;

> c. it is hard to find self-sacrificing, dedicated soul-winners like myself.

The over-anxious and dedicated national brethren have taken much of the blame for what could actually be the missionary's hunger for success. It is the national's dedication to the ministry and their willingness to sacrifice that may very well be their downfall. This dedication may be taken advantage of by the inconsiderate and disorganized missionary. The nationals sometimes take over weak works that are not properly prepared for them.

The missionary needs to see "the other side of the coin" and do the work right rather than bend to the pressure of success. The pressure of success can drive the missionary to do things that lack long-term wisdom. He must properly prepare both the church and the national pastor for a smooth, successful transition.

Clearly Defined Goals

Goals must be clearly defined, and plans must be made to achieve them. Planning goals is simply good administration, practiced by the unsaved, successful, secular organizational leaders of our day. Goals were made for man, not man for the goals. A smart man will know the goals, and a wise man will know the exceptions to the goals. To sacrifice the permanent on the altar of the immediate, for the sake of goal-keeping, would also be a disaster for the missionary's work.

The Necessity of National Leadership

Placing trained, qualified national leadership in churches will not be easy. The leadership must be trained in the fundamentals of the faith. If they are not, they could easily lead the church into the charismatic movement or neo-evangelicalism. The national leadership must be qualified, or they could easily fall prey to the sins of the flesh: money, pride, or immorality.

But unless there is adequate leadership for the beginning congregation, the trend is for it to become just one more anemic church whose growth has been thwarted because it has been prematurely turned loose from maternal influences that could have strengthened it and brought it to vigorous maturity and reproduction.

Yes, we must watch out for baby-church abuse. Unless and until the newborn congregation has the leadership of a gifted, God-called pioneer pastor, it is best to leave it with close ties to a sponsoring mother (central) church that can give the new infant a reasonable period to develop, sense the strength and support of the family and finally mature into a healthy mother in its own right, ready to assume the role of healthy parenthood of other baby churches. (Kratz, 1981, pp. 6-7)

Choosing National Leadership

The leadership of the national church must come from the church body itself. This is a biblical principle that began in Acts chapter two with the choosing of a man to take Judas's place, and in Acts chapter six with the choice of the first deacons. Later, the Apostle Paul told Timothy to train men so they could "train others also" (*II Timothy 2:2*). The natural tendency is to want to retain control of the work or the church. The missionary fears the collapse of his long years of hard work. This fear is not unfounded.

Without its own leadership, the church will always be the "American Church." As long as it is the gringo's church, he might as well pay the light and water bills. This attitude is not what the missionary wants. To avoid this attitude, the missionary must identify potential leaders and train them.

The missionary must see to it that from among the nationals there emerges at the earliest possible moment a leadership of their own. He will be associated with that leadership and that leadership with him, but he will not be the final authority and no man, either western or national should occupy that place, for final authority rests in the church and not in an individual. (Lindsell, 1965, p. 301)

Are these God's converts or the missionaries' converts? If they are God's, then the missionary needs to trust God to lead these on to maturity. There is a point at which the mother bird, having done all she could for her young, must then push them out of the nest, or they will never learn to fly. They will either starve or be devoured by predatory enemies. This push must not come until the church is ready; not until it has developed leadership that is faithful to the Lord rather than to the missionary. This kind of leadership ability results from proper training. The missionary must reproduce himself. He must reproduce his strengths rather than his weaknesses.

One does not become faithful simply by being given a spiritual responsibility. The missionary must not choose leadership that might become responsible for duty, but rather those who have been faithful through all kinds of trials and persecutions. This former kind of leadership will bring quick and possibly fatal disaster upon the national church.

The kind of leadership the new church needs can only come from those who would be faithful even when no one is watching; from those who guard their testimony in the neighborhood and pay their bills. The only kind of leadership that will build a strong national church that will not crumble at the slightest quake is that which is self-motivated and self-sustained, needing no one but God to support and approve it. God can use the national as well as the missionary, for they too are indwelt by the Holy Spirit. The missionary's great task is to bring the young church to the point where it can get along without him—to work his way out of the job.

It is not easy to be the kind of missionary-teacher who can instill in the nationals a desire to learn and lead. If it is not instilled within them, stagnation will probably set in quickly. The opportunities to teach will not come just in the classroom. The missionary's everyday life will also teach the nationals a great deal about walking with the Lord.

The difference between the pupil who works for himself and the one who works only when he is driven is too obvious to need explanation. The one is a free agent, the other is a machine. The former is attracted to his work and, prompted by his interest, works on it until he encounters overwhelming difficulty or reaches the end of his task. The latter moves when he is urged. He sees what is shown him, he hears what he is told, advances when his teacher leads, and stops just where and when the teacher stops. The one moves by his own activities, and the other by borrowed impulse. The former is a mountain stream fed by living springs, the latter a ditch filled from a pump worked by another's hand. (Milton, 1954, pp. 81-82)

Certainly, the leadership cannot be chosen from those recently saved. This choice would be against Scripture (*I Timothy 3:6*) and against good sense. The chief man must not be new in the faith. It would be better for the missionary to stay on longer at the church than to lose the labor of years by the mismanagement of a novice. It may be slower, but it will be more secure.

Paul certainly knew what he was talking about when he wrote against appointing a novice to a leadership position. He no doubt knew the danger of pride; it was the enemy's trap. Perhaps he was thinking of John Mark's departure from the work. More than a natural ability to lead is needed for leadership that will benefit the church. Years of experience just in life's trials will be helpful.

The steady advance of veterans is more powerful than the mad rush of recruits. The world's best work in the schools as in the shops is done by the calm, steady and persistent efforts of skilled workmen who know how to keep their tools sharp and make every effort reach its mark. (Milton, 1954, p. 10)

Charles H. Spurgeon had a rule at his pastoral college that remains a good principle to follow even 155 years later. He insisted that any man accepted for ministerial training have two years of effective Christian service behind him.

But it remains that the national church must be governed by national leadership. That leadership should first be presented by the missionary as possible candidates. Then the church can choose from among these. It should not be a popularity contest, and it will be up to the missionary to see that it is not. The conscientious missionary will first notice these leaders and then bring them along to the point of accepting leadership positions and continuing training.

The missionary cannot and must not make the final decision. His choice of leadership may not always be the best. He may not know the people as well as they know each other. Their wisdom, if directed, will choose the one best suited for them.

Training National Leadership

Leadership needs to be ahead of the people. It is not enough to guess which way the church is going and jump in front, saying, "Follow me, I am your leader." Training leadership is not just a matter of sending young people away to school for a couple of years. When churches are failing and are being maintained by missionaries after being turned over to the nationals, it is time to reevaluate training methods.

Training nationals to take the missionary's place may be harder than the missionary remaining in those positions himself. After all, he may have twenty-two years of good education, while the national has only three to five years. The missionary knows he could do it better himself, but he must not yield to this temptation. Yielding to this will rob the national of an opportunity to learn and grow, and to get the training he needs.

Of course it is entirely possible for the missionary himself to take the place of leadership. In some ways that is the easiest, for you have no training problems and no questions about whether the work will continue in the way you have it planned. But the poor missionary soon finds himself burdened down with responsibilities without number. And

*in spite of all his efforts the church doesn't seem to progress.
If he were to have to leave the field, as has happened, the
work would fall to pieces.* (Cook, 1954, pp. 192-193)

The missionary cannot possibly do all the work. He
could spread himself so thin that he would accomplish little.
He cannot be held responsible for the work of the other
five missionaries who did not answer God's call. If he tries
to handle this burden, he could very well have a nervous
breakdown. There is hardly anything more wasteful than
this kind of effort. The missionary is burdened and has his
heart in the right place, but he left his head in the closet
when he practices this kind of ministerial roulette. He must
delegate authority and responsibility to the nationals to
preserve his ministry as well as build an indigenous church.

*The question for him is two-fold: How can he, as quick as
possible make himself unnecessary, and how meanwhile, can
he make himself most useful to the church which eventually
will take over his responsibilities?* (Hogben, 1946, p.
147)

Allowing the nationals to do the available work is not
just a good idea; it is the best way for the missionary to
work himself out of a job. Impatience is the worst enemy,
and pride feeds this impatience. The missionary might
have difficulty accepting that the work could go on quite
well without him, perhaps even better.

The missionary needs to train others to lead singing,
give announcements, take offerings, and teach Sunday
school. If necessary, he must have training sessions for
these simple activities. These people have sat in the pew
all their lives while someone spoke Latin and served them
bread and wine. They have no idea how to participate in
the operation of the services. They will have to get over
their shyness, and sometimes that only comes by actually
rehearsing services with them.

The national church must stand on its own. The word "indigenous" means that it survives on its own. Bananas thrive in Colombia. They grow naturally, everywhere, and need no special care from outside sources. In Minnesota, a hothouse atmosphere is required for their survival. Bananas are not indigenous to Minnesota. If the controlled environment were taken away, the banana trees would die in the cold of the Northland. The national church must be planted, nurtured, and survive on the indigenous principle, or the missionary labors in vain. This building can only be done through good leadership training programs.

Indigenous principles are fast becoming the norm rather than the ideal standard. The old paternalism, and "handout" approach of the nineteenth century must be completely repudiated. Today every national group wants to be itself, independent of all other nations and especially independent of the West. We should respect this.

A missionary in the Philippines was approached by a local congregation for funds to build a church. He replied, "If I give you the money, you will have to say, 'This is the building the American gave us.'" (Fife, 1968, p. 55)

One cannot get away from the feeling that it is a fact, whoever pays the bills also "calls the shots." As long as the missionary builds the churches, schools, and camps, he will normally want to control the administration. This control causes more problems than one could imagine, especially when the missionary also pays the national's salary through a unified budget.

In 1958, the United States government offered to give financial aid to public education. Up to that date, all public education had been funded locally and controlled by a board that consisted of local people. The government offered each state a certain amount of funds, claiming that the assistance was "without strings attached." There was a great deal of debate over the matter. Now, in 1986, the federal government controls public education by threatening to cut off the flow of funds that public schools had come to depend on for their survival. [*AUTHOR NOTE: These are the dates in the original dissertation. The situation still exists as of the writing of this book.*]

The same kind of control will be imposed on the national church if the missionary insists on always supplying its needs. Sometimes, it would be better to forgo certain unnecessary programs, buildings, and equipment if the national church becomes dependent on the missionary for its supply and upkeep.

> *It was not generally a national church. It belonged to the white masters and represented a form of religious imperialism, or colonialism. It degraded the national and created within him feelings of hatred and distrust. The nationals were subjected to the indignity of "pay day" as vassals at the hand of the master when they were employed in the work of the mission. Authority rested in the hands of the missionary. Discipline came from him. (Lindsell, 1955, p. 257)*

The missionary must trust God to oversee the national church to its maturity. It is the missionary's job, through preaching, teaching, and training, to bring the congregation to a certain level of spirituality. The missionary must trust God and the biblical training he has given these people. If he has done his job correctly, they will survive.

There was a saying in the United States Navy, "It is amazing that this ship still runs quite smoothly even though the Captain and officers are ashore!" The ship only ran smoothly because the Captain had ensured it through the excellent training he gave his crew, so that in his absence, all would go according to the book.

The nationals are usually better equipped to run their

own church. Their own people do not easily fool them. They can sometimes handle their own problems much better than the missionary can even see them. Their standards could very well be higher than the missionary's and more biblical.

Releasing the Church

The releasing of churches to nationals has followed two extremes or a biblical norm. The example of the apostles is sufficient to lead the missionary down the right path for nationalization. Because of pressures from supporting churches and the mission agency, the missionary-pastor may feel under great stress to "release that church" even though it may not be ready.

Release Chart

See the release chart, called "Example of the Lord's Apostles" on the next page.

One missionary gathers a crowd with his dynamic personality and teaches people to look to and depend on him. This attitude causes the national to lean on the missionary, and he creates a "baby church" that must always be under the care of its mother.

Another missionary gathers a crowd by give-away programs and thus draws mostly women and children. When he gets a sufficient number, the missionary appoints any willing man as pastor, possibly training him on the weekends. This will establish a weak situation that could easily fall into the hands of the neo-evangelicals or the charismatic movement.

The knowledgeable missionary gathers around him born-again serious converts who are following the Lord.

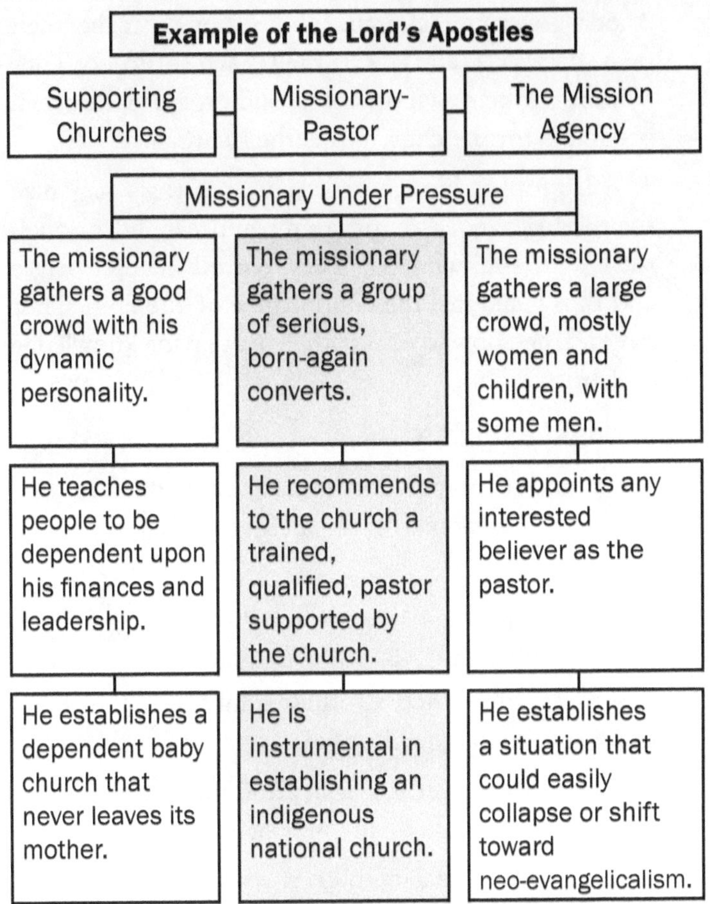

When the church is ready, the missionary suggests a qualified pastor to seek the church's approval. This man is then called and supported by the church. This third plan will establish a national church strong enough to survive the tests of time. It will be a:

1. Self-supporting church. The nationals pay for their own building and bills. They have enough tithers to cover the pastor's salary and, if necessary, fund facility expansions. The mission and the missionary are not holding the church up financially.

2. Self-governing church. The nationals make their own decisions and elect their own officers. They administer their own discipline and organize their own programs for the church. It is their church.

3. Self-propagating church. The nationals organize their own evangelistic programs and expand through their own soul-winning. They reproduce themselves and thus guarantee the continuance of the faith. They have learned how to bring others to a saving knowledge of Christ.

Preparing the Church

What kind of preparation does a church need to have to make the transition to an indigenous church? The church needs:

1. To be able to pay its own bills and have a debt-free building and parsonage.

2. At least fifteen active, tithing adults with the ability to reproduce the membership.

3. To offer the pastor a salary and parsonage at least equal to the average of the people in his church.

4. To have the capacity to carry the future load of the schools and a camp.

The Tithing Principle

The well-known principle of ten tithing families to support a church and a pastor sounds good on paper, but in reality if these ten only make the minimum salary, the offerings will fall short of meeting the needs.

Most pastors with an education would not be pleased to live on a minimum salary. For this reason, few pastors from poor sections of the country return to their home areas to minister. The church could not pay its bills, make improvements and repairs to the buildings, purchase equipment, and buy tracts or materials for the Sunday school program.

A Properly Prepared Church

What are the things to seriously consider before suggesting that the church call a national pastor?

1. Do your fellow missionaries and nationals agree that the work is ready for this big step? This is not a vote, only opinions.

2. Have the prospective pastor and the people been properly prepared for the transition?

3. Can the church meet the needs of the pastor even in times of crisis?

4. Is the parsonage well-equipped and in good condition?

5. Are the people working in the church or expecting the pastor to do it all?

Methods For Releasing the Church

What are the best ways to turn the church over to the nationals so that it will continue to grow and be strong?

1. After preparing the church as previously suggested, the church calls a pastor for six months to work with the missionary. After six months, the church ordains the national pastor, and the missionary begins to work as the pastor's assistant. Then, gradually, the missionary fades out of the picture. He takes on other duties and eventually disappears from the scene. He always remains available if called.

2. The ideal way to turn it over is never to have to turn it over. This means that one should use a national from the very beginning. This can be done in two ways:

a. A state or national missionary association made

up of missionaries and nationals sends a national pastor to a needy area, supplying his needs from the already established churches; and

b. After the missionary has built a strong church in a populated area, he stays on longer at the central church. He uses the offerings and leadership to start another church in a nearby neighborhood or city. This method would be doing it right from the start and would allow:

> i. the sponsoring church to become stronger and more missionary-minded, as they would be responsible for starting and funding the new work;

> ii. the ideal of starting a church with a national pastor from the very beginning;

> iii. the missionary family to become more settled and secure, not having to move locations as much;

> iv. the missionary-pastor has the opportunity to make good contacts in the upper class of the city, which usually takes much longer.

The Lot Bank Program

Goals

The best program for building churches is the "Lot Bank Program." The four major goals of this program are:

1. To establish churches that own sufficient land for a growing future.

2. To ensure that churches have adequate buildings.

3. To guarantee that churches have full-time pastors.

4. To create churches that can start other churches.

In this program, the missionary purchases land and

erects the initial structure at the beginning of a new work. As the Lord blesses, the congregation grows into a church that can carry on its own building programs and support a national pastor. Moral obligation and missionary vision require that this church reproduce itself by providing land of equal size and utility for another congregation.

Steps of Operation

Step One: The missionary starts the original church by purchasing lot #1 and erecting church building #1 with his own funds. Supporters in the homeland would donate these funds.

Step Two: The missionary develops the work on lot #1, and as the church grows, they use their tithes to buy lot #2 and prepare to erect a building there.

Step Three: After the building is completed on lot #2, the missionary releases the church on lot #1 to a national pastor. The missionary then begins to work in the church on lot #2.

Step Four: The missionary develops the church on lot #2 while the church on lot #1 finally receives the title deed for its property. Proper documentation is prepared to protect the local church's sovereignty.

Step Five: As the church on lot #2 grows, they are released to a national pastor when they have purchased lot #3 and erected a building. Thus, the original investment is used repeatedly to help new churches acquire land and buildings.

Advantages of the Lot Bank Program

1. Relatively inexpensive land can be purchased at the beginning of the work.

2. Funds that would have been lost in a renting situation are maintained in permanent properties.

3. Land purchased in the initial stages of development of the work is usually in a more ideal location, which could produce quicker growth.

4. The fact that facilities are owned instead of rented helps give permanence and stability to the new congregation.

5. Beginning almost immediately, the new congregation can erect a building that will meet its long-range needs.

6. Adequate facilities in the early years of development provide for the possibility of greater growth. The congregation, relatively early in its development, can organize and call a full-time pastor.

Specifications of the Lot Bank Program

Initial funds should come from some source other than the nationals. The missionary must have a church gift-loan fund. This is interest-free money loaned to erect buildings or buy land. This money must be paid back in U.S. dollars, or it will be lost in inflation and exchange rate differences. The missionary raises this money from his churches and supporters.

Initial lots should be purchased in locations with easy, familiar access. The lot should be large enough to erect a building of at least 150 square meters. The parsonage should not be in the church building, or the Sunday school classrooms will be lost.

Initial buildings should be large enough to seat a congregation of 150-200 people. Usually, a simple one-floor construction meets the need. This initial structure should be constructed in conjunction with a master building plan.

Longevity

The strongest churches in the United States are those

with long-term pastors. A pastor in the U.S. sometimes takes years to "get the ball rolling" in terms of confidence and contacts. Yet some missionaries expect to build a strong indigenous work in just a few short years. The missionary cannot expect to do this when he is:

1. Starting from nothing.

2. Working against a 95% Catholic, Muslim, Hindu, or Buddhist culture.

3. Struggling with language and culture barriers.

4. Trying to build a solid financial work on the tithes of the poor.

5. Required to return home for furlough periodically, leaving his young church in the leadership of another.

Therefore, the longevity of the missionary on a particular field is very important. His second term will be three times as productive as his first, because he will know the language and people better. A turnover of pastors will destroy any church, and a turnover of missionaries will never build strong indigenous churches on the mission field.

A call to a national pastor should be considered as a lifetime call by both the church and the pastor. One incentive for long pastorates is to offer the national the parsonage as a gift if he stays for ten years. Kind treatment such as this will produce the good interpersonal relationships that will foster church growth.

Conclusion

The missionary is to build a national church that can survive in its own environment—an indigenous church. It must reflect the national flavor with buildings and national leadership. If the missionary succeeds in making it a national church, it will survive even when he is absent from the scene.

Dr. Latham's fouth church in Gravataí, Rio Grande do Sul, Brazil.

GRAVATAÍ CITY COAT OF ARMS

CHAPTER 6
Family Life on the Mission Field

Introduction - Family-Oriented

A missionary's ministry will usually be family-oriented. He will reach families and draw families to the church. His personal family relationship could be a great blessing to the work. Most third-world countries have strong family ties, much stronger than in the United States. This does not mean that these same families know anything about biblical principles or family responsibilities as outlined in the Word of God.

The task before the missionary is difficult. Taking his family into foreign lands, which may involve very primitive, crude living conditions, does not make it any easier. When he does take his family onto foreign soil, and that family walks with the Lord, they can be a tremendous blessing and example to the nationals.

Family relationships are under great strain today. The numerous books on proper parenthood and on understanding your children are a great help. Their variety and the volume of editions testify that this is indeed a very serious problem of our day.

In 1968, Dr. Clyde Narramore took a survey of missionaries in Puerto Rico. The three greatest problems in their lives were listed in the following order: family relationships, conflicts with fellow missionaries, and cultural issues. (Narramore, 1969, N.P.)

Most missionaries are tender and compassionate people. They make good soul winners and excellent parents. They would readily admit that they would be out of line if they insisted that their children also be missionaries. Just because the children know the language perfectly and have few problems with the culture does not mean that God will automatically call them back to that field. Most missionaries, like any parents, would be satisfied if their children put Christ first and served Him faithfully.

Family Life Chart

See the "Family Life Concerns" chart on the next page.

There seem to be two extremes in how family challenges are handled on the mission field. The families that linger at either extreme will suffer some great losses. Those who practice the biblical norm are experiencing both problems and great blessings. Their few problems are only the normal ones. The principles outlined in this chart are the results of watching both extremes destroy God's families. It is with great sorrow that the extremes even have to be explained.

The missionary is under pressure from the growing amount of needy work and the limited time factor. Some missionaries work well under pressure, while others allow pressures to alter good judgment.

The missionary can work his children as an assistant pastor would, and they will usually resent it. The children may say, "My dad is all work and no play." These missionaries think that field council meetings are vacation times for the children. Their children will begin to despise the ministry.

The other extreme is to leave the children out of the ministry, possibly sending them to a boarding school on the field or even leaving them in the United States. Even

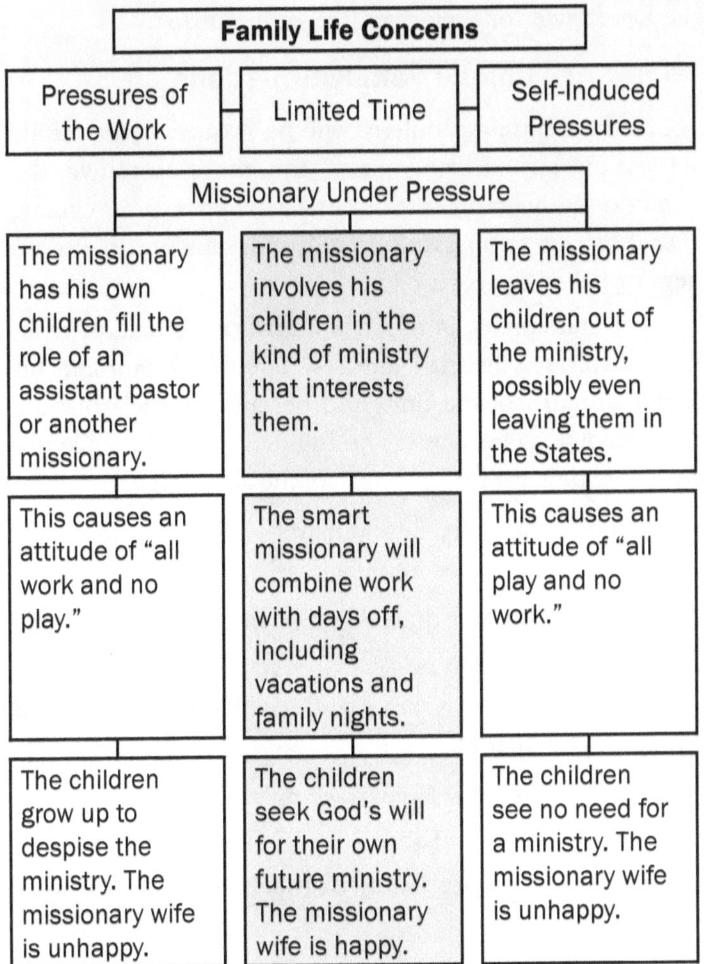

when the children are with their parents, it may be all play and no work, leaving them unable to see any real need for a ministry.

The happiest families are those that involve the children in their interests, such as puppets, music, or Daily Vacation Bible School. Some might even allow their young men to preach in the churches, developing their abilities. A good combination of work and play will lead children to seek the Lord's will for their own lives and ministry.

Unique Family Situations

Normal family problems will be greater as the family serves on any mission field; the more primitive the conditions, the more serious the problems. The climate always affects temperaments, and most mission fields are near or below the equator.

The missionary family has a different situation from most stateside Christian families. The missionary and his family are an isolated unit, and because of the isolation, they become a close unit. The following factors, while not complete deficits, bring about unique situations:

1. The missionary family may be the only Americans for a radius of 300 miles.

2. They have left their relatives and long-time friends in the homeland.

3. The only thing that may resemble their homeland would be their home.

4. The father may have his study in the home, allowing him to spend many hours within the family unit.

5. The missionary family is usually together for every meal.

This closeness can cause problems, especially when children must be separated from their families for educational reasons. While on the field, the children could study hundreds of miles away from home, and when they go to the States, it could be ten thousand miles away. Theirs is different from the usual case of homesickness; for missionary children may be separated by five to ten thousand miles from not only their beloved family but also from the country, customs, and language they have now adopted as their own. This is a unique family and a unique situation.

Each mission field will dictate different family situations. Some live in better conditions than they did in their homeland. Some educate their children at home rather than sending them abroad or to a boarding school. But each missionary must feel a great responsibility to his family. In reality, God called the husband and wife to be missionaries, not the children, but God, in His divine wisdom, also chose these children to be the offspring of missionaries.

The missionary cannot plan his children's future. He can only teach them the way they should go and leave the rest up to God. The goal of every missionary ought to be to direct his family affairs so that: his wife is loved and cherished, his children learn to love and respect both the homeland and the adopted country, his family enjoys the ministry together, and his children never regret having had to go to the mission field with their parents.

There are many casualties in missionary families. Therefore, missionaries must formulate definite ideas and lay out clear plans for the successful completion of their ministry, including family relationships.

Personal Life Habits

Travelling

Deputation means traveling many miles. Most missionaries travel as a family. The time in the car can be utilized to learn verses and songs. Each party could take his turn in choosing the next place to eat. Most missionary children have seen a great deal of their native land and possibly a good portion of the world. God blesses these missionary children. They have had advantages that others never see. Not only do they speak two languages, but they are also bi-cultural. They are very wise in geography.

They should be taught to recognize these advantages and appreciate the positive part of being in a missionary family. Travel on the field is far less than during deputation or furlough. Since there are many miles between cities of significant size, the missionary may have to travel long distances to attend field council meetings and camp, exchange money, or shop. Traveling may not always be comfortable or enjoyable. The missionary should provide for music, games, reading, sleeping quarters, and refreshment stops. If traveling by public bus, it is best to buy a seat for everyone and choose the best bus line.

Vacations

A vacation is not a luxury, but rather a farsighted investment in the longevity of one's ministry. The work can be monotonous and very tiring. The missionary needs a break from the routine.

Most missionary agencies allow their missionaries thirty days of vacation a year. Since a vacation is an excellent time to get away from the hurried pace, it would seem pointless to travel so far and hurry so much that rest is not achieved. What they do on vacation depends on their particular tastes.

Vacation may be a physical stimulus as well if the missionary works in a city where the temperature never gets below 80 degrees, and the water comes out of the ground at 155 degrees. The cooler climate of the mountains or seashore can be very refreshing.

People who think that they are showing great enthusiasm by staying at their work without a holiday are making a great mistake and one has only to look at their work to see how great that mistake is. (Hogben, 1946, p. 145)

Hobbies

The stress of the work and the pace of daily activities can drive one to the brink of nervousness. An enjoyable diversion should be scheduled into the daily routine. There are hobbies that the new environment could suggest. Examples are: collecting butterflies or arrowheads, sewing or painting, woodworking or leather-crafts, or possibly ham radio or photography. Whatever it is, it should be more relaxing than work.

Holidays

These days should be made special. Both Brazilian (national) holidays and American holidays could be observed. Customs that the children will remember should be established, such as putting up the Christmas tree on Thanksgiving Day, having tacos on Christmas Eve, or singing the "Star Spangled Banner" on the Fourth of July. Children do not find it hard to get into the spirit of things. Birthdays are family holidays. The birthday person could pick all the meals for the day and would be free from household duties.

Church Services

Families need to attend church together. On deputation, the children may sing and quote verses, and tell what they will do on the field. And when the missionary arrives on the field, they can do the same, as soon as they learn the language.

While on the field, the missionary needs to teach the nationals the importance of a strong family unit. Therefore, meetings should not be scheduled seven days a week. Scheduling meetings for the majority of the week does not necessarily demonstrate faithfulness to the Lord. It may be a quick way to ruin family relationships, especially when the unsaved (national) husband is left at home to fend for himself.

Children usually enjoy handing out tracts. Many opportunities may be found at the bus station, in supermarkets, at street meetings, or on vacation. The family should have ingrained in them a natural sense of being a witness wherever they go.

There could be other family ministries such as a puppet program, entertaining unsaved guests, sharing family slides and pictures of family experiences, and allowing the children to teach in the Sunday school or preach in the service. When Americans visit the field, the children can translate during preaching and teaching.

Family Night

The missionary will do himself a favor and a great service to his family if he plans one night a week for a family night. The family could play games for all ages, build things, play tennis, swim, or ride a motorcycle. Marking a special time for each child during the week will build a good relationship with each one. If there is something better to do during the daytime, adjust your schedule.

Education

The area of education for missionary children is fraught with significant conflicts and difficult decisions. Some cities may not have adequate schooling conditions, so the missionary must teach his children at home. (This method of teaching may be very distasteful for both the student and the unfortunate teacher.)

There are other options for children's education. Some may send their children to the public schools. In some cases, this may not be quality education, or the children might encounter many personal problems with national students and teachers. The question of whether the child is a leader or follower would help determine this option.

Sending the children away to school in a foreign field

is sometimes harder on the parents than on the children. Many missionary children have rebelled when sent away to school. The home influence and close family life are much more important than a quality education. The ideas and patterns formulated in the family will greatly influence the child's opinion of God and the ministry. The missionary's greatest gift to his children will be himself, and as much love as he can give. Besides this gift, a personal example the children can follow will be of great help.

Furlough

The entire family should be part of the presentation while on furlough. They worked and sacrificed too. Furlough time should meet the needs of the whole family. Each family member could make a list of things they want to do while on furlough, and as the family travels from church to church, the list could be followed.

If the father has to travel a great deal alone, he should make sure the time he spends with the family is quality time. Many churches enjoy seeing the whole family, and the wife will almost always be missed.

Honeymooners

Honeymooning is vital for the missionary couple. A night or two out will serve the couple well. A trip to the mountains or the seashore is one way to lift spirits. Possibly, the couple could send the children to various homes and enjoy the silence of their own home. Even the most primitive conditions do not excuse one from maintaining a close relationship with the wife of his youth.

When the children are gone, there needs to be an attractive force for the missionary couple. The missionaries cannot revolve their life around the children. They need to build a loving relationship with each other. Then, the nationals will have a pattern to follow in their marriages.

Conclusion

It would be tragic for the missionary to serve the Lord with such dedication and still fail to nurture a wholesome family relationship. One can serve the Lord, have a successful ministry, and still raise a family that loves the Lord and the ministry. It can only be done by taking the time to recognize potential trouble and taking steps to avoid it. Success in any endeavor does not come by accident.

If the missionary is trying to multiply the force, there is no better way than to bring his children up to love the Lord and appreciate the ministry. The children could even be better missionaries than their parents if they copied their parents' strengths rather than multiplying their parents' weaknesses. The greatest tribute that a missionary could hear would be, "I want a family just like the one in which I was raised."

I have fought a good fight, I have finished my course, I have kept the faith: Henceforth there is laid up for me a crown of righteousness, which the Lord, the righteous judge, shall give me at that day: and not to me only, but unto all them also that love his appearing.

2 Timothy 4:7-8

AUTHOR
- Dr. Tom Latham

1987 (DMin Graduation)   2026 (Semi-Retired)

Dr. Latham's full name is Harry Thomas Latham, but to his friends, he is Tom. His Brazilian friends know him as Pastor Thomas. He publishes under his pen name, Dr. Tom Latham. His remarkable career as a missionary in Brazil spans more than 50 years. Many factors contributed to his success, but above all, his resolute faith in Jesus Christ, his personal Savior, had the greatest impact.

Tom became a Christian while serving in the U.S. Navy, where he began holding Protestant Divine Services whenever his ship was at sea. After completing his naval service, he spent the next four years at bible college to further his spiritual journey. Graduation from Central Baptist Theological Seminary earned him a Master of Divinity (MDiv) degree. He achieved a significant milestone in his studies by earning a Doctor of Ministry

(DMin) degree from Luther Rice Seminary.

Tom met Penny Stimpson, and together they began a mission to serve God in Brazil. Their family grew to include three children, six grandchildren, and ten great-grandchildren. Together, they started four churches in Brazil.

Tom led extremely successful wrestling programs in many public schools for more than 20 years, including training and coaching. His church team won the Brazilian National Title in 2010 and the State title in 2013.

Although Penny was promoted to glory, Tom continues to serve Christ in Brazil.

Read many details about Dr. Latham and his educational journey at www.brazilwrestler.com.

God had an only Son and He made Him a missionary.

David Lingingstone, 19th-Century Missionary

This is the last photo of the entire Latham family, taken in 2023, a few months before Penny was carried by angels into the arms of her loving Savior.

Back Row: Thomas, Kossette, and Shane.
Front Row: Penny and Tom.

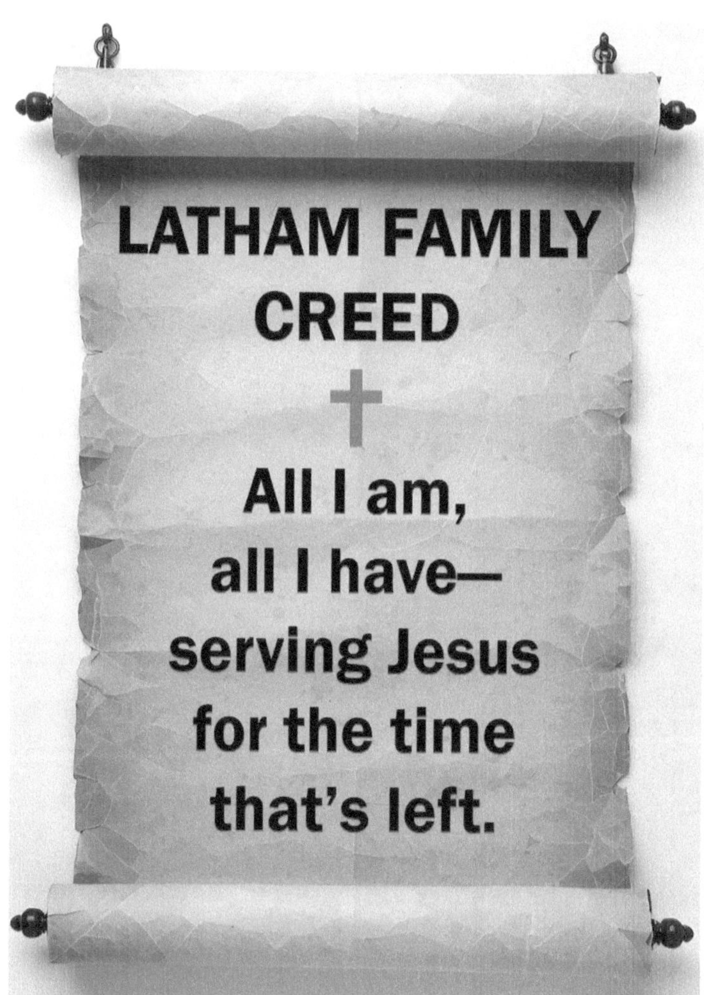

LATHAM FAMILY CREED
All I am,
all I have—
serving Jesus
for the time
that's left.

BIBLIOGRAPHY

[*AUTHOR NOTE: This dissertation was completed in 1987, thus the dates of these references reflect that time period.*]

Adams, Jay E., *Competent to Counsel: Introduction to Nouthetic Counseling*. Grand Rapids: Zondervan Publishing House, 1970.

Allen, Roland. *Missionary Methods: Saint Paul's or Ours?* Grand Rapids: William & Eerdmans Publishing Company, 1962.

Amstutz, Harold. *Missionary Principles and Practices.* (Association of Baptists for World Evangelism), N.D.

Asher, James J . "Fear of Foreign Languages," *Psychology Today*. August 1981, pages 52-58.

Bowely, Eric. "Training Them to Train Their Own," *Good News Broadcaster.* July/August, 1982, page 38.

Carver, William Owen. *The Course of Christian Missions.* New York: Fleming H. Revell Company, 1939.

Caudill, R. Paul . *A Minister Looks at His World.* Nashville: Broadman Press, 1975.

Coggins, Wade T. *So That's What Missions Is All About.* Chicago: Moody Press, 1975.

Cook, Harold R. *An Introduction to the Study of Christian Missions*. Chicago: Moody Press, 1954.

_____. *Counseling Cross-Culturally*. Grand Rapids: Zondervan Publishing House, 1984.

Dye, T. Wayne. "Stress-Producing Factors in Cultural Adjustment," *Missiology: An International Review*. 1974, Vol. 2, Issue 1, pp. 61-77.

Fife, Eric S. and Arthur F. Glasser. *Missions in Crisis*. Downers Grove, IL: Zondervan Publishing House, 1978.

Gregory, John Milton. *The Seven Laws of Teaching*. Grand Rapids: Baker Book House, 1954.

Hesselgrave, David J. *Communicating Christ Cross-Culturally*. Grand Rapids: Zondervan Publishing House, 1978.

Hillis, Dick. "Milk, Men and Miracles," *Moody Monthly*. January 1983, pages 96-98.

Hiscox, Edward T. *The New Directory For Baptist Churches*. Chicago: The Judson Press, 1894.

Hogben, Rowland. *Missionary in Training*. Chicago: InterVarsity Christian Fellowship, 1946.

Isais, Juan. *The Other Side of the Coin*. Grand Rapids: William B. Eerdmans Publishing Company, 1966.

Kratz, James. "Watch Out For Child Abuse," *World Mission*. April 1981, pages 6-7.

LaHaye, Tim. *The Battle For The Family*. Old Tappin, New Jersey: Fleming H. Revell Company, 1982.

Lewis, Norman. *"Go Ye" Means You*. Lincoln, Nebraska:

Back to the Bible Publishers, 1962.

Lindsell, Harold. *Missionary Principles and Practices*. New York: Fleming H. Revell Company, 1955.

Lutzer, Erwin. "Failure in the Ministry," *Moody Monthly*. January 1983, pages 83-84.

Mayers, Allen. *Christianity Confronts Culture*. Grand Rapids: Zondervan Publishing House, N.D.

Metzger, Richard A. "The Local Church - A Sending Authority," *Good News Broadcaster*. April 1981, pages 44-46.

Narramore, Clyde M. *Problems Missionaries Face*. Grand Rapids: Zondervan Publishing House, 1969.

Orr, James. Editor. *International Standard Bible Encyclopedia*. Grand Rapids: William B. Eerdmans Publishing Company, 1939.

_____. *Planting Churches Cross-Culturally*. Grand Rapids: Zondervan Publishing House, 1984.

Richardson, Don. "How Missionaries Enrich Cultures," *Moody Monthly*. June 1976, pages 55-58.

Robertson, A. T. *Word Pictures in the New Testament*. Nashville, Tenn.: Broadman Press, 1930.

Rossen, Betty. "Skippy, Skillets and Sports Illustrated," *His*. January 1982, pages 9-11.

Savage, Robert. *At Your Orders, Lord!* Grand Rapids: Zondervan Publishing House, 1957.

Smith, Gorden Hedderly. *The Missionary and Anthropology*. Chicago: Moody Press, 1945.

Soltau, Stanley T. *Missions at the Crossroads*. Grand Rapids:

Baker Book House, 1954.

Sorley, Wilber S. "Missionary Temperament Under Field Tensions." Assam, India: N.P., 1963.

Strachan, Kenneth R. *The Inescapable Calling*. Grand Rapids: William B. Eerdmans Publishing Company, 1968.

Trueblood, Elton. *The Validity of the Christian Mission*. New York: Harper & Row, 1972.

Williamson, Mabel. *Have We No Rights?* Chicago: Moody Press, 1957.

INDEX

D

E

Evangelism Chart 98
evangelistic heart 8
Evangelistic meetings 92
Example of the Lord's Apostles 114

F

faith in Christ 97
Family Life Chart 124
Family Night 130
family-oriented 123
Family relationships 123
fear of failure 43
Field Work and Tensions 55, 56
Fighting Stress 44
final crisis 14
First Impressions 6
Flexibility 42
Fractured interpersonal relationships 31
friendship evangelism 91
Frustration 42, 43, 44
Fundamental Baptist ix
fundamentals 106
furlough 14, 59, 103, 104, 105, 121, 128, 131

G

give-away programs 114
Goal of Evangelism 84
Goals 106, 118
God ix, 2, 4, 6, 8, 10, 12, 14, 21, 26, 27, 31, 32, 33, 34, 36,
     37, 38, 39, 43, 45, 49, 51, 52, 53, 54, 55, 57, 58, 59,
     61, 74, 79, 81, 82, 83, 85, 86, 87, 90, 93, 94, 95, 96,
     97, 98, 99, 100, 106, 107, 108, 111, 113, 123, 124,
     127, 131, 134
Going National 9
Good Relationships 57
Government Dealings 25
Great Commission 81

H

health problems 28
Helping Suggestions 78

Tithing 75, 116
Total Discipleship Chart 90
Total Discipleship Program 89
tracts 91, 117, 130
Training 110, 137, 138
Training National Leadership 110
Transit Authorities 19
Travelling 127

U

Ultimate Goal of Evangelism 84
Unique Family Situations 126

V

Vacations 128

W

way of thinking 18
well-adjusted missionary 3
Word of God 32, 81, 83, 87, 93, 100, 123
world evangelism 81
worms 15, 20, 21
wrestling 134

Books by
Dr. Tom Latham

www.brazilwrestler.com/book/

AUTOBIOGRAPHY

Exceptional opportunity to examine a 50-year professional journey, brought to life through 130+ vibrant color images.
Into the Light: Half-Century as Missionaries in Brazil
(ISBN 978-1-885708-19-9)

Other Books

Brazilian Adventures (ISBN 978-1-885708-25-0)
Missionary Problem Areas (ISBN 978-1-885708-27-4)

SHANE WOODS SERIES

1: *The Snow Peak Robbers* (ISBN 978-1-885708-51-9)
2: *The Strawberry Fair* (ISBN 978-1-885708-52-6)
3: *The Buzzard Butte Poachers* (ISBN978-1-885708-53-3)
4: *The Eastern Rodeo* (ISBN 978-1-885708-54-0)
Planned for 2026-2027
5: *The Linn County Vandals*
6: *The Nez Perce Treasure*
7: *The Mountain Lion*
8: *The Precarious Plane Ride*
9: *The Empty Coffin Mystery*
10: *The State Championship*
11: *The Baseball Problem*